Congressional
Research Service

Informing the legislative debate since 1914 _____

Federal Contracting and Subcontracting with Small Businesses: Legislation in the 113th Congress

Kate M. Manuel
Legislative Attorney

May 30, 2014

Congressional Research Service

7-5700

www.crs.gov

R43573

Summary

Congress has generally broad authority to impose requirements upon the federal procurement process (i.e., the process whereby agencies acquire supplies and services from other entities for the agency's direct benefit or use). One of the many ways in which Congress has exercised this authority is by enacting measures that encourage agencies to contract and subcontract with "small businesses." For purposes of federal procurement law, the term *small business* generally denotes a business that (1) is independently owned and operated, (2) is not dominant in its field of operations, and (3) has fewer employees or annual receipts than the standards that the Small Business Administration (SBA) has established for the industries in which the business operates.

In exercising its authority over procurement, Congress has declared a policy of ensuring that a "fair proportion" of federal contract and subcontract dollars is awarded to small businesses. It has also required the executive branch to establish government-wide and agency-specific goals for the percentage of contract and/or subcontract dollars awarded to small businesses that equal or exceed specified percentages of federal procurement spending (e.g., 3% for Historically Underutilized Business Zone (HUBZone) small businesses). Congress has similarly required or authorized agencies to conduct *set-asides*, or competitions in which only small businesses may compete, as well as to make noncompetitive or "sole-source" awards to small businesses in circumstances when such awards could not be made to other businesses. In addition, the SBA and officers of the procuring agencies are tasked with reviewing and restructuring proposed procurements to maximize opportunities for small business participation.

Congress periodically amends the statutes governing contracting and subcontracting with small businesses to further its declared policy of ensuring that small businesses receive a "fair proportion" of federal procurement spending. The 111th and 112th Congresses, in particular, made numerous changes to such statutes. These Congresses enacted legislation (P.L. 111-240, P.L. 112-239) that addresses, among other things, (1) the standards under which business size is determined; (2) goals for contracting and subcontracting with small businesses; (3) prime contractors' obligations in subcontracting with small businesses; (4) SBA guarantees of small businesses' performance and payment bonds; (5) "bundling" and "consolidation" of agency requirements into contracts unsuitable for performance by small businesses; (6) set-asides for women-owned small businesses; and (7) mentor-protégé programs for small business contractors.

Compared to the 111th and 112th Congresses, the 113th Congress has enacted or introduced relatively few measures addressing small business contracting to date, perhaps because the amendments made by its predecessors are still being implemented and assessed. Many of the measures that have been enacted or introduced address goals for contracting or subcontracting with small businesses (P.L. 113-66, H.R. 2441, H.R. 2550, H.R. 2551, H.R. 4093, S. 196, S. 258, S. 1190). Several measures also address bundling and consolidation (H.R. 2550, H.R. 2551, H.R. 2694, H.R. 4094, H.R. 4435, S. 1304); prime contractors' obligations in subcontracting with small businesses (P.L. 113-66, H.R. 2551, H.R. 4093, S. 196, S. 259); and agency-specific contracting programs, like the Department of Veterans Affairs' "Veterans First" program (H.R. 2719, H.R. 2882, H.R. 3098, H.R. 4228, H.R. 4435, S. 1893, S. 2334). Other measures address when agencies may make set-aside or sole-source awards to small businesses (H.R. 489, H.R. 2358, H.R. 2452, H.R. 2550, H.R. 2551, H.R. 4281, H.R. 4435, S. 99, S. 206, S. 430, S. 1607, S. 2334). Additional measures address other topics (P.L. 113-66, P.L. 113-76, H.R. 776, H.R. 1622, H.R. 2750, H.R. 2751, H.R. 4228, H.R. 4435, S. 523).

Contents

Tables

Contacts

ongress has generally broad authority to impose requirements upon the federal procurement process (i.e., the process whereby agencies acquire supplies and services from other entities for the agency's direct benefit or use).[1] One of the many ways in which Congress has exercised this authority is by enacting measures that encourage agencies to contract and subcontract with "small businesses." For purposes of federal procurement law, the term *small business* generally denotes a business that (1) is independently owned and operated, (2) is not dominant in its field of operations, and (3) has fewer employees or annual receipts than the standard that the Small Business Administration (SBA) has established for the industry in which the business operates.[2]

In exercising its authority over procurement, Congress has declared a policy of ensuring that a "fair proportion" of federal contract and subcontract dollars is awarded to small businesses.[3] It has also required the executive branch to establish government-wide and agency-specific goals for the amount of contract and/or subcontract dollars awarded to small businesses that equal or exceed specified percentages of federal procurement spending (e.g., 3% to Historically Underutilized Business Zone (HUBZone) small businesses).[4] Congress has similarly required or authorized agencies to conduct *set-asides*, or competitions in which only small businesses may compete, as well as to make noncompetitive or "sole-source" awards to small businesses in circumstances when such awards could not be made to other businesses.[5] In addition, the SBA and officers of the procuring agencies are tasked with reviewing and restructuring proposed procurements to maximize opportunities for small business participation.[6] CRS Report R42391, *Legal Authorities Governing Federal Contracting and Subcontracting with Small Businesses*, by Kate M. Manuel and Erika K. Lunder, discusses these and related measures in more detail.

---

[1] *See, e.g.*, Perkins v. Lukens Steel Co., 310 U.S. 113, 127 (1940) ("Like private individuals and businesses, the Government enjoys the unrestricted power to produce its own supplies, to determine those with whom it will deal, and to fix the terms and conditions upon which it will make needed purchases."). However, the U.S. Constitution does impose certain limits upon Congress's power in this regard, most notably by guaranteeing all persons equal protection of the law. U.S. Const. amend. V (guaranteeing due process of law); Bolling v. Sharpe, 347 U.S. 497 (1954) (finding that due process under the Fifth Amendment includes equal protection, or the constitutional assurance that the government will apply the law equally to all people and not improperly prefer one class of people over another). Equal protection issues arise most frequently with contracting preferences based on race or gender. Race and gender are "suspect classifications," which means that the government must demonstrate that any programs that classify individuals on this basis are narrowly tailored to further a compelling government interest, in the case of race-conscious programs, or substantially related to important government objectives, in the case of gender-conscious programs. *See, e.g.*, Adarand Constructors, Inc. v. Peña, 515 U.S. 200 (1995) ("strict scrutiny" applied to program that classified individuals on the basis of race); Craig v. Boren, 429 U.S. 190, 197 (1976) ("intermediate scrutiny" applied to program that classified individuals on the basis of sex).

[2] 15 U.S.C. §632(a).

[3] *See* 15 U.S.C. §631(a) ("It is the declared policy of the Congress that the Government should aid, counsel, assist, and protect, insofar as is possible, the interests of small-business concerns in order to preserve free competitive enterprise, to insure that a fair proportion of the total purchases and contracts for property and services for the Government ... be placed with small-business enterprises, to insure that a fair proportion of the total sales of Government property be made to such enterprises, and to maintain and strengthen the overall economy of the Nation.").

[4] *See, e.g.*, 15 U.S.C. §644(g)(2) (requiring agencies, in consultation with the SBA, to set goals for the percentage of federal contract and/or subcontract dollars awarded to small businesses that "realistically reflect" the ability of small businesses to perform such contracts and subcontracts).

[5] *See, e.g.*, 15 U.S.C. §657a (authorizing set-asides and sole-source awards to HUBZone small businesses).

[6] *See, e.g.*, 15 U.S.C. §634(b)(11) (requiring the SBA to appoint Procurement Center Representatives (PCRs) to work with the procuring agencies); 13 C.F.R. §125.2(b) (requiring PCRs to review all acquisitions not set aside for small businesses to determine whether a set-aside is appropriate and to identify alternate strategies to maximize small business participation as contractors or subcontractors, among other things).

Congress periodically amends the statutes governing contracting and subcontracting with small businesses to better achieve its declared policy of ensuring that small businesses receive a "fair proportion" of federal procurement spending. The 111th and 112th Congresses, in particular, made numerous changes. These Congresses enacted legislation (P.L. 111-240, P.L. 112-239) that addresses, among other things, (1) the standards under which business size is determined; (2) goals for contracting and subcontracting with small businesses; (3) prime contractors' obligations in subcontracting with small businesses; (4) SBA guarantees of small businesses' performance and payment bonds; (5) "bundling" and "consolidation" of agency requirements into contracts unsuitable for performance by small businesses; (6) set-asides for women-owned small businesses; and (7) mentor-protégé programs for small business contractors.[7] Compared to the 111th and 112th Congresses, the 113th Congress has enacted or introduced relatively few measures addressing small business contracting to date, perhaps because the amendments made to the various laws governing small business contracting by its predecessors are still being implemented and assessed.

This report describes, by issue area, the various small business contracting bills in the 113th Congress and, particularly, the modifications to existing law that they have made, or would make if enacted. In doing so, the report also briefly surveys current law on particular issues pertaining to small business contracting and subcontracting, including significant amendments to current law made by the 111th and 112th Congresses. The latter information is included because, in many cases, the legislation proposed in the 113th Congress would build on changes made by its predecessors.[8] Although the report cites numerous bills, it does not attempt to include all legislation related to small business contracting in the 113th Congress. Nor does it discuss all provisions of bills that are included. Rather, its focus is upon legislation that reflects distinctive approaches to issues in small business contracting (e.g., increasing goals, authorizing set-asides or sole-source awards). The report will be updated as additional legislation is enacted or introduced.

Government-Wide and Agency-Specific Goals

Government-wide and agency-specific goals for the percentage of contract and/or subcontract dollars awarded to small businesses have long been part of the federal procurement process. Congress amended Section 15(g) of the Small Business Act in 1978 to require that agency heads, in consultation with the SBA, set *agency-specific goals* for the percentage of federal contract and subcontract dollars awarded to small businesses each year.[9] Ten years later, in 1988, Congress further amended Section 15(g) to require the President to set *government-wide goals* for the percentage of federal contract and/or subcontract dollars awarded annually to various categories of small businesses.[10] These government-wide goals must equal or exceed certain percentages

---

[7] For further discussion of these and other changes made by the 111th and 112th Congresses, see generally CRS Report R42390, *Federal Contracting and Subcontracting with Small Businesses: Issues in the 112th Congress*, by Kate M. Manuel and Erika K. Lunder.

[8] *See, e.g., infra* notes 26-29 and accompanying text.

[9] An Act to Amend the Small Business Act and the Small Business Investment Act of 1958, P.L. 95-507, §221, 92 Stat. 1770-1771 (Oct. 24, 1978) (codified at 15 U.S.C. §644(g)(2)). These agency-specific goals must "realistically reflect the potential" of small businesses to perform agency contracts and subcontracts. 15 U.S.C. §644(g)(2)(A)-(B). They must also "present ... the maximum practicable opportunity" for small businesses to participate in agency contracts, and the cumulative prime contract goals for all agencies must meet or exceed the annual government-wide goal established by the President. 15 U.S.C. §644(g)(1)(B).

[10] Business Opportunity Development Reform Act (BODRA), P.L. 100-656, §502, 102 Stat. 3881 (Nov. 15, 1988) (continued...)

---

specified in statute (currently, 23% of federal contract dollars awarded to small businesses (of any type);[11] 5% of federal contract and subcontract dollars awarded to women-owned small businesses; 5% to small businesses owned and controlled by "socially and economically disadvantaged" individuals and groups;[12] 3% to HUBZone small businesses; and 3% to service-disabled veteran-owned small businesses).[13] Individual contracts may be counted toward multiple goals. For example, an award to a HUBZone small business counts toward both that goal and the overall small business goal.

The 1978 and 1988 amendments granted the executive branch considerable discretion in determining how the "total value of all prime contract and subcontract awards" for a fiscal year was to be calculated,[14] and in deciding what steps should be taken to meet the government-wide and agency-specific goals. This discretion, coupled with persistent failures to meet the goals,[15] prompted the 111th and 112th Congresses to make multiple changes to what is commonly known as the "Small Business Goaling Program." Initially, the 111th Congress required that senior procurement executives, senior program managers, and agency directors of Small and Disadvantaged Business Utilization (OSDBUs) communicate to their subordinates the "importance of achieving small business goals."[16] Subsequently, the 112th Congress reiterated this requirement,[17] and made other amendments to Sections 15(g) and (h) of the Small Business Act with the intent of improving performance of these goals. Among other things, the 112th Congress directed the SBA to review its "Goaling Guidelines" to ensure that certain types of spending are not excluded when goals are set.[18] It also imposed several requirements as to the establishment of

---

(...continued)

(codified, as amended, at 15 U.S.C. §644(g)(1)).

[11] Under federal law, some types of small businesses, or their owners, must meet certain socioeconomic criteria (e.g., women-owned, located in a HUBZone). Others need only be small. The contracting preferences for the latter firms are more limited than those for the former. *See infra* **Table 1**.

[12] For more on who qualifies as "socially and economically disadvantaged" for purposes of federal procurement law, see CRS Report R40987, *"Disadvantaged" Small Businesses: Definitions and Designations for Purposes of Federal and Federally Funded Contracting Programs*, by Kate M. Manuel.

[13] 15 U.S.C. §644(g)(1)(A)(i)-(v).

[14] The SBA historically used its discretion to exclude certain contracts from these calculations, such as contracts performed outside the United States and contracts awarded through the Javits-Wagner-O'Day (JWOD) Program (providing for federal procurement from workshops employing people who are "blind or severely disabled"). *See, e.g.*, Small Business Goaling Report: Fiscal Year 2010, *available at* https://www.fpds.gov/downloads/top_requests/FPDSNG_SB_Goaling_FY_2010.pdf (listing exclusions); Small Bus. Admin., Office of Inspector General, Small Business Administration's Rationale for Excluding Certain Types of Contracts from the Annual Small Business Procurement Calculations Needs to be Documented, Advisory Memorandum Report No. 12-04, Dec. 6, 2011.

[15] *See, e.g.*, Charles S. Clark, Agencies Report Slight Progress in Meeting Small Business Contracting Goals, *Gov't Exec.*, July 2, 2013, *available at* http://www.govexec.com/contracting/2013/07/agencies-report-slight-progress-meeting-small-business-contracting-goals/65987/ (noting that the SBA reported "progress" toward meeting the goals in FY2012, but that the goals were not met); Jeff Kinney, SBA Notes Drop in Small Business Contract Awards for FY2011, 98 *Fed. Cont. Rep.* 27 (July 10, 2012).

[16] Small Business Jobs Act, P.L. 111-240, tit. I, subtitle C, §1333, 124 Stat. 2542 (codified at 15 U.S.C. §644(g)(2)(F)(i)-(ii)).

[17] National Defense Authorization Act for FY2013, P.L. 112-239, §1631(b), 126 Stat. 2070-2073 (Jan. 2, 2013).

[18] *Id*. at §1631(b), 126 Stat. 2072. Specifically, under P.L. 112-239, the SBA must ensure that agency goals are established in a manner that does not exclude certain categories of contracts based on the type of goods or services acquired; or, in the case of certain contracts subject to competitive procedures, based on whether the contract is subject to the Federal Acquisition Regulation (FAR), or whether funding is made directly available by an appropriation or by reimbursement from another agency or account. The SBA must also ensure that agency subcontracting goals are established on the basis of "realistically achievable improvements" in levels of subcontracting, rather than on the basis (continued...)

---

agency-specific contracting goals,[19] directed agencies to take specified steps to meet their goals,[20] and increased reporting regarding goaling program performance.[21] In addition, the 112th Congress mandated an independent assessment of the goaling program[22] and required that certain members of the Senior Executive Service (SES) be trained on contracting requirements under the Small Business Act.[23]

Legislation Enacted by the 113th Congress

Building on the work of its predecessors, the 113th Congress has also addressed the government-wide and agency-specific goals for contracting and subcontracting with small businesses. One measure enacted by the 113th Congress amended Section 15(h) to require that agency reports regarding performance in contracting and subcontracting with small businesses include a "remediation plan with proposed new practices to better meet such goals, including analysis of factors leading to any failure to achieve such goals."[24] Previously, such plans only had to address (1) the extent of small business participation in agency contracts and subcontracts, (2) whether the agency achieved its goals, and (3) justifications for any failures to attain goals.[25]

Another measured enacted by the 113th Congress amended Section 15(g) to permit the Department of Energy (DOE) to count *first-tier subcontracts* awarded by contractors managing and operating national laboratories toward the DOE and government-wide goals for *prime contracts*.[26] This change arguably reflects the unique nature of the supplies and services the DOE purchases, a sizeable percentage of the total value of which is made up of contracts for the management and operation of laboratories that are generally seen as unsuitable for performance by small businesses. At earlier dates, the DOE had prime contract goals that were substantially lower than those of other agencies.[27] However, the DOE could potentially have been said to have failed to comply with certain requirements imposed by the 112th Congress—particularly a requirement that agencies "make a consistent effort to annually expand participation by small

---

(...continued)

of previous years' performance, and that agencies document the basis for any decision to establish a goal that is lower than the government-wide goal for small businesses in that category. *Id.*

[19] *Id.* at §1631(b), 126 Stat. 2071 (requiring that agencies separately address prime and subcontract awards for each category of small businesses (e.g., women-owned) in their goals, and make a "consistent effort to annually expand participation" by small businesses in each category).

[20] P.L. 112-239, §1631(b)(2), 126 Stat. 2071 (codified at 15 U.S.C. §644(g)(2)(D)-(F)).

[21] P.L. 112-239, §1632, 126 Stat. 2073-2076.

[22] *Id.* at §1631(d), 126 Stat. 2072-2073. This assessment must address certain topics, such as the industrial composition of companies receiving federal prime contracts and subcontracts; the industrial composition of domestic small business concerns; barriers to accurately capturing data on small business contracting and subcontracting; and recommendations for improving the quality and availability of data regarding small business contracting. It is separate from, but to be "coordinated with," the assessment of the contracting performance of the Department of Defense required under Section 1613 of P.L. 112-239.

[23] P.L. 112-239, §1633, 126 Stat. 2076.

[24] National Defense Authorization Act for FY2014, P.L. 113-66, §1613, 127 Stat. 948 (Dec. 26, 2013) (codified at 15 U.S.C. §644(h)(1)(D)).

[25] 15 U.S.C. §644(h)(1)(A)-(C).

[26] Consolidated Appropriations Act, P.L. 113-76, §318,—Stat.—(Jan. 17, 2014).

[27] *See, e.g.*, Small Business Admin., Small Business Procurement Scorecards, Department of Energy, 2007, *available at* http://www.sba.gov/sites/default/files/files/doe_assessment_07.pdf (last accessed: May 12, 2014) (reporting a goal of awarding 4.34% of prime contract dollars to small businesses).

---

business concerns from each industry category in [agency] procurement contracts and subcontracts"[28]—if it had reported this same low goal as to prime contracts year after year, without any increases. Counting certain subcontracts as if they were prime contracts arguably gives the DOE greater latitude for improvements in its performance as to its prime contracting goals. On the other hand, an argument could be made that treating subcontracts as if they were prime contracts minimizes the DOE's incentives to contract with small businesses. Those opposed to counting certain DOE subcontracts as prime contracts may also note that subcontractors do not enjoy the same protections as prime contractors under federal law, making it inappropriate to equate the two.[29]

Legislation Proposed in the 113th Congress

Members of the 113th Congress have also introduced legislation that would increase the government-wide goals for the percentage of contract and/or subcontract dollars awarded to small businesses, thereby also effectively increasing the agency-specific goals.[30] Most commonly, these measures would increase the goal for the percentage of prime contract dollars awarded to small businesses (of any type) from 23% to 25%, and the goals for the percentage of contract and subcontract dollars awarded to small disadvantaged businesses and women-owned small businesses from 5% to 10% each.[31] Some measures would also increase the goals for the percentage of contract and subcontract dollars awarded to HUBZone small businesses and service-disabled veteran-owned small businesses from 3% to 5%-6% each.[32] Such measures respond to concerns that the current goals—which were set a decade or more ago—are too low and do not adequately reflect the availability of minority-, women-, and service-disabled veteran-owned small businesses in today's marketplace.[33] Also, given recent reports that the federal government has met its goals for contracting and subcontracting with small businesses for the first time in seven years,[34] an argument could be made that increasing the goals is necessary to ensure continued federal efforts and improvements in this area.

---

[28] *See* 15 U.S.C. §644(g)(2)(D).

[29] For further discussion, see generally CRS Report R41230, *Legal Protections for Subcontractors on Federal Prime Contracts*, by Kate M. Manuel.

[30] *See* 15 U.S.C. §644(g)(1)(B) ("The Small Business Administration and the Administrator for Federal Procurement Policy shall ... insure that the cumulative annual prime contract goals for all agencies meet or exceed the annual Governmentwide prime contract goal established by the President pursuant to this paragraph.").

[31] *See, e.g.*, Minority Small Business Enhancement Act, H.R. 2550, §4(a); Expanding Opportunities for Main Street Act, H.R. 2551, §104(a); Assuring Contracting Equity Act, S. 196, §2(a)(1)-(2); House Rules Committee Amendment No. 56, to H.R. 4435, as passed by the House, House of Representatives Committee on Rules, H.R. 4435, *available at* http://rules house.gov/bill/113/hr-4435; House Armed Services Committee, FY15-H.R. 4435 Floor Amendments and Tracker, *available at* http://armedservices house.gov/index.cfm?p=fy15-h-r-4435-floor-amendments-and-tracker. *See also* Greater Opportunities for Small Business Act, H.R. 4093, §2(a) (increasing only the goal for small businesses generally, from 23% to 25%).

[32] *See, e.g.*, Assuring Contracting Equity Act, S. 259, §2(a)(3).

[33] *See, e.g.*, *Doing Business with the Government: The Record and Goals for Small, Minority, and Disadvantaged Businesses: Hearing Before the Subcommittee on Economic Development, Public Buildings, and Emergency Management of the Committee on Transportation and Infrastructure, House of Representatives, 110th Cong., 2d Sess.*, at 1 (Mar. 6, 2008). The most recently established statutory goal is that for contracting with service-disabled veteran-owned small businesses, which was set in 1999. The goals for contracting with other types of small businesses were established at earlier dates.

[34] *See, e.g.*, J.D. Harrison, *Government on Pace to Meet Small Business Contracting Goal—But Will the Bar Get Higher?*, WASH. POST, *available at* http://www.washingtonpost.com/business/on-small-business/government-on-pace-to-meet-small-business-contracting-goal—but-will-the-bar-get-higher/2014/02/26/d3ba6e98-9ef5-11e3-9ba6-(continued...)

Other measures introduced in the 113th Congress would clarify how particular contracts are to be counted for goaling purposes. Several of these measures seek to prevent "double dipping," or counting a single contract toward multiple goals because, for example, it happens to be awarded to a firm that is owned by a service-disabled woman that is participating in the SBA's Minority Small Business Ownership and Capital Development Program (commonly known as the "8(a) Program").[35] These measures would generally bar agencies from counting a small business in more than two categories (e.g., HUBZone, women-owned) when determining whether the agency has met its goals.[36] Some measures would also require agencies to count awards to small businesses participating in the 8(a) Program toward the goal for small disadvantaged businesses, as opposed to other goals.[37] Other measures would clarify how specific contracts (e.g., contracts with "teaming arrangement entities") are to be counted.[38]

Yet other bills in the 113th Congress would mandate reporting of specific information about agencies' performance in contracting and subcontracting with small businesses, or would require independent assessments of agency performance.[39] Other measures would repeal the provisions, previously noted, that authorize the DOE to count first-tier subcontracts awarded by management and operations contractors toward the DOE and government-wide prime contracting goals.[40]

(...continued)

800d1192d08b_story html (last accessed: May 12, 2014).

[35] For more on the 8(a) Program, see generally CRS Report R40744, *The "8(a) Program" for Small Businesses Owned and Controlled by the Socially and Economically Disadvantaged: Legal Requirements and Issues*, by Kate M. Manuel.

[36] *See, e.g.*, Minority Small Business Enhancement Act, H.R. 2550, §4(b); Expanding Opportunities for Main Street Act, H.R. 2551, §104(b); Assuring Contracting Equity Act, S. 196, §2(b).

[37] *See, e.g.*, Assuring Contracting Equity Act, S. 196, §2(b). All 8(a) participants are small disadvantaged businesses, but not all small disadvantaged businesses are 8(a) participants. *See generally* CRS Report R40987, *"Disadvantaged" Small Businesses: Definitions and Designations for Purposes of Federal and Federally Funded Contracting Programs*, by Kate M. Manuel.

[38] *See, e.g.*, Small Business Fairness Act, H.R. 2441, §2; & S. 1190, §2 (expressly permitting agencies to count contracts with "teaming arrangement entities" toward their goals if a small disadvantaged business, HUBZone small business, woman-owned small business, or service-disabled veteran-owned small business "performs" the teaming arrangement entity's obligations under the contract); Assuring Contracting Equity Act, S. 196, §3 (requiring that agencies count the value of each prime contract awarded per year, regardless of whether the contract is awarded as the result of unrestricted competition or any SBA determination regarding small businesses' potential to perform). This provision is somewhat modified in the later bill of the same name (i.e., S. 259). *See infra* note 39.

[39] *See, e.g.*, Minority Small Business Enhancement Act, H.R. 2550, §4(c) (requiring the Government Accountability Office (GAO) to report on "disparities" in the award of contracts to small disadvantaged businesses, small businesses, and other firms); Assuring Contracting Equity Act, S. 259, §3 (requiring the SBA to include in its reports on goaling performance "the total value of all prime contract awards for a fiscal year, including the value of each prime contract awarded for the fiscal year, without regard to whether the prime contract was awarded as the result of unrestricted competition or any determination by the Administrator with respect to the potential for a small business concern to perform the prime contract or a subcontract under the prime contract").

[40] Greater Opportunities for Small Business Act, H.R. 4093, §2(a) (repealing Section 15(g)(3) of the Small Business Act); House Rules Committee Amendment No. 56, to H.R. 4435, as passed by the House, House of Representatives Committee on Rules, H.R. 4435, *available at* http://rules.house.gov/bill/113/hr-4435; House Armed Services Committee, FY15-H.R. 4435 Floor Amendments and Tracker, *available at* http://armedservices house.gov/index.cfm?p=fy15-h-r-4435-floor-amendments-and-tracker.

Subcontracting Plans

The basic requirement that agencies incorporate clauses stating U.S. policy as to subcontracting with small businesses into their prime contracts, and "subcontracting plans" into larger prime contracts, originated with the 1978 amendments to Section 8(d) of the Small Business Act.[41] As amended, Section 8(d) generally requires agencies to incorporate terms addressing subcontracting with small businesses in contracts performed within the United States whose *value exceeds a minimum threshold (currently, generally $150,000).*[42] These terms (1) articulate that it is the "policy of the United States" that small businesses have the "maximum practicable opportunity to participate" in the performance of federal contracts, and (2) obligate the prime contractor to carry out this policy "to the fullest extent consistent with the efficient performance of th[e] contract."[43] In addition, *"larger" contracts (currently those whose value exceeds $650,000 ($1.5 million for construction contracts))* that offer subcontracting possibilities must generally also incorporate so-called subcontracting plans with

- percentage goals for the amount of work to be subcontracted with various types of small businesses (e.g., HUBZone small businesses);

- descriptions of the efforts the contractor will take to ensure that small businesses have "an equitable opportunity to compete" for subcontracts;

- assurances that the contractor will "flow down" these requirements to all subcontractors (other than small businesses) with "larger" subcontracts (currently, those valued in excess of $650,000 ($1.5 million for construction contracts)); and

- recitations of the types of records the contractor will maintain to demonstrate the procedures it has adopted to comply with its subcontracting plan.[44]

Recent Congresses have, however, made a number of amendments to Section 8(d), in part, because of concerns about agencies' performance in meeting the government-wide and agency-specific goals for contracting and subcontracting with small businesses.[45] Initially, the 111th Congress amended Section 8(d) in an attempt to address "bait-and-switch" (i.e., prime contractors using subcontractors other than those whom they said in their bid or offer that they would use), and subcontractors' difficulties in obtaining payment from prime contractors. Among other things, the 111th Congress required that subcontracting plans include terms obligating prime contractors to make "good faith efforts" to obtain supplies and services from the small businesses they "used" in preparing their bids and proposals, and provide the contracting officer a written explanation if they do not.[46] It also required prime contractors to notify the contracting officer in writing if they

---

[41] *See* P.L. 95-507, §211, 92 Stat. 1767-1770 (codified, as amended, at 15 U.S.C. §637(d)).

[42] 15 U.S.C. §637(d)(2)-(3).

[43] 15 U.S.C. §637(d)(2)-(3). Subsequently, Section 8(d) was further amended to articulate that it is also the "policy of the United States" that subcontractors be "timely paid" for their work. *See* 15 U.S.C. §637(d)(3)(A).

[44] 15 U.S.C. §637(d)(6)(A)-(H). The regulations implementing Section 8(d) require contractors to agree to some additional terms as part of their subcontracting plans, including the total dollars planned to be subcontracted and the total dollars planned to be subcontracted to small businesses, as well as the principal supplies and services to be subcontracted. *See* 48 C.F.R. §19.704(a)(2)-(3).

[45] *See supra* note 15 and accompanying text.

[46] P.L. 111-240, §1322, 124 Stat. 2540-2541 (codified at 15 U.S.C. §637(d)(6)(G)(i)). The SBA regulations implementing P.L. 111-240 have adopted an arguably narrow interpretation of when a prime contractor can be said to (continued...)

---

pay a "reduced price" to a subcontractor for completed work, or if payment to a subcontractor for work for which the agency has paid the prime contractor is more than 90 days past due.[47]

Subsequently, the 112th Congress imposed additional requirements on the collection and reporting of data regarding prime contractors' performance of their subcontracting plans.[48] It also provided statutory authority for contracting officers to consider prime contractors' performance in subcontracting with small businesses when evaluating their "past performance" for source-selection purposes.[49] In addition, it established further protections for subcontractors by requiring that (1) offerors who intend to identify a particular small business as a potential subcontractor in their bid or proposal notify the small business prior to doing so, and (2) the SBA establish a mechanism whereby subcontractors can report "fraudulent activity or bad faith" by contractors with respect to subcontracting plans.[50]

Legislation Enacted by the 113th Congress

The 113th Congress expanded on these requirements by enacting legislation that imposes certain obligations on prime contractors whose subcontractors are also required, through the "flow down" of contract requirements, to have subcontracting plans.[51] Among other things, the 113th

(...continued)

have "used" a small business in preparing its bid or proposal. These regulations deem such "use" to have occurred only when: (1) the offeror references the small business as a subcontractor in the bid or proposal, or associated small business subcontracting plan; (2) the offeror has a subcontract or agreement in principle to subcontract with a small business to perform a portion of the specific contract; or (3) the small business drafted a portion of the bid or proposal, or the offeror used the small business's pricing or cost information, or technical expertise, in preparing the bid or proposal, and there is written evidence of an intent or understanding that the small business would be awarded a subcontract for the related work if the offeror is awarded the contract. *See* Small Bus. Admin., Small Business Subcontracting: Final Rule, 79 Fed. Reg. 42390, 42405 (July 16, 2013) (codified at 13 C.F.R. §125.3(c)(3)(i)-(iii)).

[47] P.L. 111-240, at §1334, 124 Stat. 2542-2543 (codified at 15 U.S.C. §637(d)(12)). P.L. 111-240 also requires contracting officers to consider the "unjustified failure" of a prime contractor to make full or timely payment to a subcontractor when evaluating the contractor's performance. *Id.* However, Section 8(d) does not expressly require that these payment-related provisions be incorporated into agency contracts, and the regulations implementing Section 8(d) do not appear to require their incorporation. *See generally* 48 C.F.R. Subpart 19.7.

[48] P.L. 112-239, §1653(a)(2) & (b), 126 Stat. 2081-2083.

[49] *Id.* at §1653(a)(3), 126 Stat. 2082 (codified at 15 U.S.C. §637(d)(9)) ("The failure of any contractor or subcontractor to comply in good faith with [a required subcontracting plan] ... may be considered in any past performance evaluation of the contractor."). Prior to the enactment of this statutory provision, the Federal Acquisition Regulation (FAR) expressly required agencies to consider prime contractors' performance in subcontracting with small businesses in bundled solicitations that offered "significant" opportunities for subcontracting, and also authorized its consideration in other negotiated procurements. *See* 48 C.F.R. §15.304(a)-(b) (2010) (requiring the use of evaluation factors that "[r]epresent the key areas of importance and emphasis ... and [s]upport meaningful comparison"); 48 C.F.R. §15.304(c)(3)(ii) (bundled solicitations). Negotiated procurements are procurements wherein the government selects the vendor(s) based on factors that include, but are not limited to, price. *See generally* 48 C.F.R. Part 15. For more on bundling, see *infra* Bundling and Consolidation.

[50] P.L. 112-239, at §1653(a)(5), 126 Stat. 2082 (codified at 15 U.S.C. §637(d)(14)-(15)).

[51] *See* 15 U.S.C. §637(d)(6)(D) (requiring the "flow down" of subcontracting plan requirements to subcontractors at any "tier" (other than small businesses) holding subcontracts valued in excess of $650,000 ($1.5 million for construction contracts)). The term "flow down" is commonly used to describe the practice of requiring contractors, as terms of their contracts, to impose certain terms on their own contractors, as terms of these contractors' contracts. It is important to note, however, that only parties in privity of contract, or having direct contractual relationships with one another, are generally entitled to enforce a contract's terms. *See, e.g.*, Williams v. Fenix & Scisson, 608 F.2d 1205 (9th Cir. 1979). Subcontractors are often spoken of as belonging to various "tiers," depending upon whether their contracts are with the prime contractor (i.e., first-tier subcontractors), a contractor who has a contract with the prime contractor (continued...)

Congress required that prime contractors (and any subcontractors whose own subcontractors have subcontracting plans) review and approve their subcontractors' plans; monitor subcontractor compliance with these plans; ensure subcontracting reports are submitted when required; compare subcontractors' performance to the plans and goals; and discuss performance "when necessary" to ensure a "good faith effort" to comply.[52] The 113th Congress also required that subcontracting plans contain a recitation of all "records" that the prime contractor will maintain to demonstrate the procedures it has adopted to ensure that its subcontractors comply with their subcontracting plans.[53] In addition, the 113th Congress addressed when and how lower tier subcontracts may be counted toward prime contractors' subcontracting goals.[54]

Legislation Introduced in the 113th Congress

Other legislation in the 113th Congress would amend Section 8(d) to require that the goals for subcontracting with various types of small businesses included in subcontracting plans be "not less than 40 percent,"[55] rather than being left to agencies' discretion. Such legislation is intended to promote subcontracting with small businesses, as are other measures introduced in the 113th Congress. One bill would, for example, require the SBA to "collaborate" with contracting agencies to include contract terms that would provide contractors with "additional consideration"—an apparent reference to payment—if they meet their goals for subcontracting with small disadvantaged businesses.[56] Another bill would require the Administrator of the SBA to consult with other agency heads to develop and implement "standards" whereby contracting officers may consider potential contractors' prior performance as to their subcontracting plans when making source-selection determinations.[57] Currently, the Small Business Act authorizes consideration of this information,[58] and the Federal Acquisition Regulation (FAR) even requires it

---

(...continued)

(i.e., second-tier subcontractors), etc.

[52] P.L. 113-66, at §1614(a)(1), 127 Stat. 948.

[53] *Id.* at §1614(a)(1), 127 Stat. 948-949. Previously, subcontracting plans had to contain recitations of all records the prime contract would maintain to demonstrate *its own* compliance with the subcontracting plan, not its *subcontractors'* compliance.

[54] *Id.* at §1614(a)(4), 127 Stat. 949 (permitting prime contractors to receive credit for small businesses performing as subcontractors, at any tier, pursuant to subcontracting plans required under Section 8(d), if the subcontracting goals pertain "only to a single contract with [an] executive agency," but not if the goals pertain to a contract with more than one agency, or multiple contracts with one or more agencies). Another bill in the 113th Congress includes similar provisions as to the crediting of subcontracts, but also contains other provisions that were not enacted as part of P.L. 113-66. *See generally* Make Every Small Business Count Act, H.R. 2232, §3 (requiring the GAO to study the feasibility of using existing systems, such as the eSRS (Electronic Subcontracting Reporting System, http://www.esrs.gov/), to attribute subcontractors to specific contracts in the case of contractors with plans that pertain to multiple contracts or agencies).

[55] *See, e.g.*, Greater Opportunities for Small Business Act, H.R. 4093, §2; House Rules Committee Amendment No. 56, to H.R. 4435, as passed by the House, House of Representatives Committee on Rules, H.R. 4435, *available at* http://rules.house.gov/bill/113/hr-4435; House Armed Services Committee, FY15-H.R. 4435 Floor Amendments and Tracker, *available at* http://armedservices.house.gov/index.cfm?p=fy15-h-r-4435-floor-amendments-and-tracker.

[56] *See* Expanding Opportunities for Main Street Act, H.R. 2551, §105. The FAR currently authorizes agencies to provide similar "monetary incentives" to prime contractors whose performance in subcontracting with small disadvantaged businesses exceeds their goals. *See generally* 48 C.F.R. §19.1203.

[57] *See* Assuring Contracting Equity Act, S. 196, §4; & S. 259, §4.

[58] 15 U.S.C. §637(d)(9) ("The failure of any contractor or subcontractor to comply in good faith with [a required subcontracting plan] ... may be considered in any past performance evaluation of the contractor.").

---

in certain circumstances.[59] However, neither the Small Business Act nor the FAR prescribes specific "standards" for contracting officers to use in considering contractors' past performance in subcontracting with small businesses, such as those contemplated by the proposed legislation.

Bundling and Consolidation

The way in which agencies structure their contracting requirements can have significant implications for small businesses. When multiple requirements are grouped into a single contract, that contract may be difficult, or impossible, for small businesses to perform. For this reason, Congress has enacted progressively more stringent limitations upon the "bundling" and "consolidation" of requirements by federal agencies. First, in 1997, Congress amended the Small Business Act to define *bundling* as,

> consolidat[ing] 2 or more procurement requirements for goods or services previously provided or performed under separate smaller contracts into a solicitation of offers for a single contract that is likely to be unsuitable for award to a small business concern due to— (A) the diversity, size, or specialized nature of the elements of performance specified; (B) the aggregate dollar value of the anticipated award; (C) the geographical dispersion of the contract performance sites; or (D) any combination of the factors described in subparagraphs (A), (B), and (C),

and to require agencies to take certain steps to ensure that any bundling that they engage in is "necessary and justified."[60] Then, in 2003, Congress amended the Armed Services Procurement Act (ASPA) to prohibit defense agencies from executing any acquisition strategy that includes a "consolidation" of contract requirements valued in excess of $5 million (later adjusted for inflation to $6 million) without first (1) conducting market research, (2) identifying any alternative contracting approaches that would involve a lesser degree of consolidation of contract requirements, and (3) determining that the consolidation is necessary and justified.[61] The 111th Congress subsequently imposed similar requirements upon other agencies' contracts valued in excess of $2 million.[62] It also required (1) the development of a government-wide policy

---

[59] *See* 48 C.F.R. §15.304(c)(3)(ii). The FAR would also generally authorize the consideration of this information in cases where it is not required. *See generally* 48 C.F.R. §15.304(a)-(b).

[60] Small Business Reauthorization Act of 1997, P.L. 105-135, §§411-417, 111 Stat. 2617-2620 (Dec. 2, 1997) (codified, as amended, at 15 U.S.C. §632(o) & 15 U.S.C. §644(e)). Among other things, agencies must engage in market research before carrying out an acquisition strategy that could lead to a bundling of contract requirements to determine whether such bundling or consolidation is "necessary and justified." 15 U.S.C. §644(e)(2)(A). *Market research* describes the process of "collecting and analyzing information about capabilities within the market to satisfy agency needs." 48 C.F.R. §2.101. Part 10 of the FAR generally addresses the conduct of market research.

[61] National Defense Authorization Act for FY2004, P.L. 108-136, div. A, tit. VIII, §801(a)(1), 117 Stat. 1538 (Nov. 24, 2003) (codified, as amended, at 10 U.S.C. §2382 (2006)). Both the definition of *consolidation* and that of *bundling* refer to the grouping of two or more requirements for supplies or services that were previously provided or performed under separate smaller contracts into a solicitation of offers for a single contract. However, the definition of *bundling* expressly describes the grouped requirements as "unsuitable" for performance by small businesses, while the definition of *consolidation* does not. *See* 15 U.S.C. §657q(a)(2) ("[T]he term 'consolidation of contract requirements', with respect to contract requirements of a Federal agency, means a use of a solicitation to obtain offers for a single contract or a multiple award contract (A) to satisfy 2 or more requirements of the Federal agency for goods or services that have been provided to or performed for the Federal agency under 2 or more separate contracts lower in cost than the total cost of the contract for which the offers are solicited; or (B) to satisfy requirements of the Federal agency for construction projects to be performed at 2 or more discrete sites.").

[62] P.L. 111-240, §1313, 124 Stat. 2538-2540 (Sept. 27, 2010). Initially, the $2 million threshold would have applied to (continued...)

---

regarding bundling, (2) listings of and justifications for bundled contracts, and (3) periodic reports on the performance of agency officials who are tasked with minimizing bundling and promoting contracting with small businesses.[63] Most recently, the 112th Congress repealed the consolidation-related provisions of the ASPA and generally subjected defense agencies to the same requirements as civilian agencies.[64]

Legislation Introduced in the 113th Congress

Measures introduced in the 113th Congress would either place further limitations on bundling or consolidation of contracts, or improve reporting about bundled and consolidated contracts. The former type of measure generally seeks to amend the definition of *bundling of contract requirements* so that it applies to requirements for construction (as the definition of *consolidation of contract requirements* currently does), as well as in situations where an agency adds a new requirement to requirements previously provided or performed under separate smaller contracts.[65] These measures would also generally alter—and establish a statutory basis for—current regulatory and other procedures for resolving differences of opinion between the SBA and the procuring agency as to whether particular procurements are bundled.[66]

In contrast, measures of the second type (i.e., addressing reporting) would not alter the substantive requirements as to bundling or consolidation, but rather seek to ensure that the data

---

(...continued)

defense agencies only until the SBA certified that they were in compliance with the government-wide contracting goals under Section 15(g) of the Small Business Act, after which time the higher threshold under Title 10 would have applied. *Id.* at §1313(a), 124 Stat. 2539. However, the 112th Congress deleted these provisions when it repealed the consolidation-related provisions in Title 10. *See* P.L. 112-239, §1671(c)(2), 126 Stat. 2085.

[63] *Id.* at §1312, 124 Stat. 2537-2538.

[64] P.L. 112-239, §1671(c)(1), 126 Stat. 2084.

[65] *See, e.g.*, Minority Small Business Enhancement Act, H.R. 2550, §3; Expanding Opportunities for Main Street Act, H.R. 2551, §103. In the past, at least one agency has asserted that requirements for construction are, per se, new requirements and are not encompassed by the definition of *bundling*. *See* Tyler Construction Group v. United States, 83 Fed. Cl. 94, 100-101 (2008). At least one agency has also argued that the addition of any new requirement, which was not previously performed under a separate smaller contract, means that the requirements are not bundled. *See* Nautical Eng'g, Inc., B-309955 (Nov. 7, 2007) (agency asserting that there was no bundling because of the addition of a new requirement for planning services to the admittedly consolidated requirements pertaining to drydock and dockside maintenance and repair). There appears to be some precedent for the former argument in SBA regulations treating construction requirements as new for purposes of statutory and regulatory provisions that preclude agencies from obtaining supplies or services previously provided through or accepted for the 8(a) Program from non-8(a) firms unless the SBA authorizes them to do so. *See* 13 C.F.R. §124.504(c)(1)(ii)(B) ("Construction contracts, by their very nature (e.g., the building of a specific structure), are deemed new requirements."). The merits of the latter argument are unclear. The GAO did not address them in *Nautical Engineering* because it found that any bundling was justified since the government would receive measurably substantial benefits from the bundled solicitation.

[66] *See, e.g.*, Minority Small Business Enhancement Act, H.R. 2550, §3 (authorizing the Administrator of the SBA to delay the solicitation process for up to 10 days, and submit the matter to the OMB, whenever the SBA and the procuring agency disagree as to whether a solicitation is bundled). This time period is shorter than that currently provided for by the FAR. However, the procuring agency, not the SBA, presently determines whether any such delay occurs. *See* 48 C.F.R. §19.505 (generally providing for the issuance of a solicitation to be delayed for 15 days, so that the SBA may make a written appeal to the secretary or agency head, who has 30 days to respond). The proposed legislation would also write into statute OMB's role in mediating bundling-related disagreements between the SBA and the procuring agencies, a role that is currently prescribed by Executive Order 13170. *See* Executive Order 13170, Increasing Opportunities and Access for Disadvantaged Businesses, 65 Fed. Reg. 60827, 60829 (Oct. 12, 2000) (authorizing the SBA or the procuring agency to "seek assistance" from the OMB in cases where there is disagreement as to the existence or extent of bundling).

---

available regarding bundled and consolidated contracts is accurate and reliable. Such measures reflect concerns about the quality of federal procurement data generally,[67] and data about bundled and consolidated contracts in particular.[68] Among other things, these measures would require the Administrator of the SBA, in consultation with other federal officials, to develop a "plan" for "improv[ing] the quality of data reported on bundled and consolidated contracts" that would, among other things, (1) establish "consequences" for failure to properly identify contracts as bundled or consolidated and (2) require "periodic and statistically valid data verification and validation."[69] The plan would have to be implemented within a specified time frame, and used in compiling certain reports.[70] The Government Accountability Office (GAO) would also be required to assess the "effectiveness" of the plan and its implementation, including whether contracts are "accurately labeled" as bundled or consolidated.[71] Currently, agencies are required to identify bundled and consolidated contracts in the Federal Procurement Data System-Next Generation (FPDS-NG), and Chief Acquisition Officers must annually certify that prior year FPDS-NG records are "accurate and complete."[72] However, existing certification requirements are not specifically concerned with bundling and consolidation, and there do not appear to be any "consequences" for failure to identify bundled or consolidated contracts.[73]

Other measures introduced in the 113th Congress would address bundling and consolidation within the context of strategic sourcing. *Strategic sourcing* commonly describes the process of using analyses of an organization's spending to acquire frequently procured items more economically and efficiently.[74] The General Services Administration (GSA) has recently promoted government-wide strategic sourcing as a way to save money.[75] Individual agencies have also developed their own agency-specific strategic sourcing initiatives for the same purpose.[76] On the other hand, small businesses have expressed concern that strategic sourcing could diminish opportunities for small businesses to obtain and perform federal contracts, since small businesses may not be able to supply the large quantities of supplies and services that are often required for

---

[67] *See, e.g.*, Gov't Accountability Office, Improvements Needed to the Federal Procurement Data System-Next Generation, GAO-05-960R (Sept. 27, 2005).

[68] *See, e.g.*, Gov't Accountability Office, Impact of Strategy to Mitigate Effects of Contract Bundling on Small Business Is Uncertain, GAO-04-454 (June 28, 2004); Gov't Accountability Office, Limited Information Available on Contract Bundling's Extent and Effects, GGD-00-82 (May 18, 2000).

[69] *See, e.g.*, Contracting Data and Bundling Accountability Act, H.R. 4094, §2; National Defense Authorization Act for FY2015, H.R. 4435, as reported in the House, at §813.

[70] H.R. 4094, §2; H.R. 4435, §813.

[71] H.R. 4094, §2; H.R. 4435, §813.

[72] *See, e.g.*, GSA Federal Procurement Data System-Next Generation (FPDS-NG) Data Element Dictionary, Version 1.4.4, June 28, 2013, at pp. 99-102, *available at* https://www.fpds.gov/downloads/Version_1.4.4_specs/ FPDSNG_DataDictionary_V1.4.4.pdf ; Exec. Office of the Pres., OMB, Improving Federal Procurement Data Quality: Guidance for Annual Verification and Validation, May 31, 2011, at pg. 1, *available at* http://www.whitehouse.gov/ sites/default/files/omb/procurement/memo/improving-data-quality-guidance-for-annual-verification-and-validation-may-2011.pdf.

[73] The proposed legislation does not specify what form these "consequences" might take, apparently leaving this to agency discretion. *See* H.R. 4094, §2; H.R. 4435, §813.

[74] *See* Ralph C. Nash, Jr., Steve L. Schooner, Karen R. O'Brien-DeBakey, and Vernon J. Edwards, *The Government Contracts Reference Book: A Comprehensive Guide to the Language of Procurement* 549-550 (3d ed. 2007).

[75] GSA, Federal Strategic Sourcing Initiative, *available at* http://www.gsa.gov/portal/content/112561?utm_source= FAS&utm_medium=print-radio&utm_term=fssi&utm_campaign=shortcuts (last accessed: May 13, 2014).

[76] Gov't Accountability Office, Strategic Sourcing: Improved and Expanded Use Could Save Billions in Annual Procurement Costs, GAO-12-919, Oct. 4, 2012 (discussing initiatives at various federal agencies).

---

discounted pricing.[77] Several measures introduced in the 113th Congress would respond to these concerns by requiring the Office of Management and Budget (OMB) to develop guidance on strategic sourcing that "reflect[s] the requirements of the Small Business Act, including the provisions regarding contract bundling, contract consolidation, and the need to achieve the statutory small business prime contracting and subcontracting goals in section 15 of that Act."[78] Other measures would require the collection of data regarding strategic sourcing,[79] or independent assessments of strategic sourcing's effects on small businesses.[80]

Set-Asides and Sole-Source Awards under the Small Business Act

Competition is generally valued in federal contracting because it can result in the government paying lower prices, ensure some degree of transparency and accountability, and help prevent fraud.[81] Because of this, Congress has generally required that agencies obtain "full and open competition through the use of competitive procedures" when awarding contracts,[82] and defined *full and open competition* to mean that all responsible sources are permitted to submit bids or offers.[83] However, in keeping with its declared policy of ensuring that small businesses obtain a "fair proportion" of federal procurement dollars, Congress has also enacted a number of statutes that require or authorize agencies to use other than full-and-open competition when contracting with small businesses.[84] In particular, various provisions of the Small Business Act permit

---

[77] *See, e.g.*, Jason Miller, SBA Finds Fault with GSA's Strategic Sourcing Analysis for Office Supplies, FEDERAL NEWS RADIO, Apr. 7, 2014, *available at* http://www.federalnewsradio.com/522/3597975/SBA-finds-fault-with-GSAs-strategic-sourcing-analysis-for-office-supplies.

[78] Buy Smarter and Save Act, H.R. 2694, §3(c)(6); & S. 1304, §3(c)(6).

[79] *See* DHS Acquisition Accountability and Efficiency Act, H.R. 4228, §104 (tasking the Department of Homeland Security's Chief Acquisition Office with collecting baseline data and establishing performance measures regarding strategic sourcing's effects on small business).

[80] House Rules Committee Amendment No. 250, to H.R. 4435, as passed by the House, House of Representatives Committee on Rules, H.R. 4435, *available at* http://rules.house.gov/bill/113/hr-4435; House Armed Services Committee, FY15-H.R. 4435 Floor Amendments and Tracker, *available at* http://armedservices house.gov/index.cfm? p=fy15-h-r-4435-floor-amendments-and-tracker (GAO study).

[81] *See generally* CRS Report R40516, *Competition in Federal Contracting: A Legal Overview*, by Kate M. Manuel.

[82] *See generally* 10 U.S.C. §2304(a)(1)(A) & 41 U.S.C. §3301(a)(1). There are certain exceptions to these requirements, including when particular circumstances exist that would allow the use of other than competitive procedures (e.g., single source for supplies or services; urgent and compelling circumstances make compliance with the competition requirements contrary to the public interest). *See, e.g.*, 10 U.S.C. §2304(c) & 41 U.S.C. §3304(a).

[83] 41 U.S.C. §107. For more information on the "responsibility" requirements applicable to prospective federal contractors, see CRS Report R40633, *Responsibility Determinations Under the Federal Acquisition Regulation: Legal Standards and Procedures*, by Kate M. Manuel.

[84] 15 U.S.C. §637(a) (set-asides for small businesses owned and controlled by socially and economically disadvantaged individuals and groups); 15 U.S.C. §637(m) (set-asides for women-owned small businesses); 15 U.S.C. §644(a) (set-asides for small businesses not belonging to any other category); 15 U.S.C. §657a (set-asides for HUBZone small businesses); 15 U.S.C. §657f (set-asides for service-disabled veteran-owned small businesses). Set-asides for small businesses under the authority of Section 15(a) of the Small Business Act and its implementing regulations have been found to be mandatory because the relevant provisions of the act and regulations use the word "shall," and "shall" has been construed to indicate mandatory agency action when used in this context. *See, e.g.*, DNO Inc., B-406256, B-406256.2 (Mar. 22, 2012); Metasoft, LLC, B-402800 (July 23, 2010). However, set-asides for specific types of small businesses under other provisions of the Small Business Act have been viewed as discretionary because the statutory and regulatory provisions authorizing them use the word "may."

---

agencies to award contracts to small businesses on a set-aside or sole-source basis if certain requirements are met, as **Table 1** illustrates. Key among these requirements is that the contracting officer reasonably expects bids or offers will be received from at least two small businesses, and the award can be made at a fair market price. This requirement is commonly known as the "Rule of Two" because of its focus upon receipt of bids or offers from at least two small businesses.[85] The Department of Veterans Affairs (VA) has separate statutory authority, beyond that provided in the Small Business Act, to make set-aside and sole-source awards to service-disabled veteran-owned small businesses and other veteran-owned small businesses, as discussed below.[86]

Because legislation pertaining to the so-called "set-aside programs" for different types of small businesses (e.g., HUBZone, women-owned) has historically been enacted separately, each program is discussed below under its own heading. However, there have been occasional measures that affect set-asides or sole-source awards for all types of small businesses. These latter measures are grouped together under the heading "General."

Table 1. Set-Aside Programs for Various Types of Small Businesses

Program & Authority	Eligibility Requirements	Types of Preferences
Small businesses not belonging to any other type P.L. 85-536, §15(a), 72 Stat. 395 (July 18, 1958) (codified, as amended, at 15 U.S.C. §644(a))	Must qualify as "small" under the Small Business Act	Set-asides of contracts whose value exceeds the simplified acquisition threshold (generally $150,000) if the Rule of Two is satisfied
Small disadvantaged businesses participating in the 8(a) Program P.L. 95-507, §202, 92 Stat. 1761-1763 (Oct. 24, 1978) (codified, as amended, at 15 U.S.C. §637(a))	At least 51% unconditionally owned and controlled by one or more socially and economically disadvantaged individuals or groups (i.e., Alaska Native Corporations, Community Development Corporations, Indian tribes, Native Hawaiian Organizations) who are of good character and citizens of the United States Demonstrated potential for success	Sole-source awards of contracts valued below $4 million ($6.5 million for manufacturing contracts), or contracts valued in excess of these amounts if the Rule of Two is not satisfied[a] Set-asides of contracts valued in excess of $4 million ($6.5 million for manufacturing contracts)[a]
Historically Underutilized Business Zone (HUBZone) small businesses P.L. 105-135, tit. VI, §602(b)(1)(B), 111 Stat. 2629 (Dec. 2, 1997) (codified, as amended, at 15 U.S.C. §657a)	At least 51% unconditionally and directly owned and controlled by U.S. citizens Principal office in a HUBZone (e.g., census tracts or non-metropolitan counties with higher than average unemployment, or lower than average median incomes; lands within Indian reservations; base closure areas) At least 35% of employees reside in a	Set-asides of contracts whenever the Rule of Two is satisfied Sole-source awards of contracts valued below $4 million ($6.5 million for manufacturing contracts) if the Rule of Two is not satisfied Price evaluation adjustments of up to 10% for HUBZone firms in unrestricted competitions[b]

---

[85] For more on the Rule of Two, see generally CRS Legal Sidebar WSLG329, The "Rule of Two" and Small Business Set-Asides, by Kate M. Manuel.

[86] *See infra* VA's "Veterans First" Contracting Program. It is important to note that the Small Business Act does not authorize set-asides or sole-source awards for firms owned by veterans who are not service-disabled, unlike the Veterans Benefits Act.

Program & Authority	Eligibility Requirements	Types of Preferences
	HUBZone	
Women-owned small businesses P.L. 106-554, tit. VIII, §811, 114 Stat. 2763A–708 (Dec. 21, 2000) (codified, as amended, at 15 U.S.C. §637(m))	At least 51% unconditionally and directly owned and controlled by one or more women who are U.S. citizens In order to be considered economically disadvantaged, women's personal net worth must generally be less than $750,000 (excluding ownership interests in the concern and equity interests in primary personal residences)	Set-asides of contracts whose value exceeds the simplified acquisition threshold (generally $150,000) for firms owned by economically disadvantaged women in industries where women are underrepresented (or for firms owned by non-economically disadvantaged women in industries where women are substantially underrepresented), if the Rule of Two is satisfied
Service-disabled veteran-owned small businesses P.L. 108-183, tit. III, §308, 117 Stat. 2662 (Dec. 16, 2003) (codified, as amended, at 15 U.S.C. §657f)	At least 51% unconditionally and directly owned and controlled by one or more service-disabled veterans	Set-asides of contracts whenever the Rule of Two is satisfied Sole-source awards of contracts valued below $3.5 million ($6 million for manufacturing contracts) if the Rule of Two is not satisfied

Source: Congressional Research Service, based on the sources cited in **Table 1**.

a. Firms owned by Alaska Native Corporations, Indian Tribes, and, in the case of Department of Defense procurements, Native Hawaiian Organizations are eligible for sole-source awards under somewhat different conditions. *See generally* CRS Report R40744, *The "8(a) Program" for Small Businesses Owned and Controlled by the Socially and Economically Disadvantaged: Legal Requirements and Issues,* by Kate M. Manuel.

b. This means that, in determining which offer has the lowest price or represents the "best value" for the government, agencies may add up to 10% to the price of all offers except (1) offers from HUBZone small businesses that have not waived the evaluation preference and (2) otherwise successful offers from small business concerns. *See* 48 C.F.R. §52.219-4(b)(i)-(ii).

General

Although the various provisions of the Small Business Act requiring or authorizing set-asides or sole-source awards to small businesses each pertain to a particular type of small business (e.g., HUBZone, women-owned), in some cases, Congress has enacted or considered legislation that would affect the ability of all types of small businesses to obtain awards under these authorities. Perhaps the most notable example is legislation enacted by the 111th Congress that expressly authorizes agencies to set aside all or part of "multiple-award contracts" for small businesses.[87] A *multiple-award contract* is a single contract awarded to multiple vendors, each of which is generally entitled to a "fair opportunity to be considered" for orders valued in excess of $3,000.[88] Prior to the enactment of P.L. 111-240, the setting aside of multiple-award *contracts* for small

---

[87] P.L. 111-240, §1331, 124 Stat. 2541 (codified at 15 U.S.C. §644(r)) (requiring the promulgation of regulations authorizing agencies to (1) "set aside part or parts of a multiple award contract" for small businesses; (2) place orders against multiple-award contracts without giving all contractors a fair opportunity to be considered for such awards; and (3) "reserve 1 or more contract awards for small business concerns under full and open multiple award procurements").

[88] 10 U.S.C. §2304c(b) (procurements of defense agencies); 41 U.S.C. §4106(c) (procurements of civilian agencies). The Federal Acquisition Streamlining Act (FASA) of 1994 established a "preference" for multiple-award contracts by requiring agencies to use them, as opposed to single-award contracts, "to the maximum extent practicable." *See* P.L. 103–355, tit. I, §1004(a)(1), 108 Stat. 3249 (Oct. 13, 1994) (codified, as amended, at 10 U.S.C. §2304a(d)(3)) & *id.* at tit. I, §1054(a), 108 Stat. 3261 (codified, as amended, at 41 U.S.C. §4103(d)(4)(A)).

businesses seems to have been an accepted practice. However, there was not express statutory authority for such set-asides. Even more significantly, an argument could be made that the setting aside of *orders* under multiple-award contracts was prohibited because of provisions of federal law which generally require that all vendors holding a multiple-award contract have a "fair opportunity to be considered" for orders under the contract.[89] The legislation enacted by the 111th Congress vitiates this argument by expressly permitting set-asides of orders "notwithstanding the fair opportunity requirements," as well as other set-asides and reservations of parts of multiple-award contracts.[90] This legislation also defines *multiple award contract* in a way that apparently encompasses Federal Supply Schedule contracts.[91] Previously, questions had been raised about the applicability of set-asides to Schedules contracts.[92]

Several measures introduced by Members of the 113th Congress would similarly affect the ability of all types of small businesses to obtain set-aside contracts. For example, one measure would provide that "timely offers" from Federal Prison Industries (FPI)—a government-owned corporation that sells products manufactured by federal prisoners to federal agencies—are not to be considered if the contract has been set-aside for small businesses under "section 15(a) of the Small Business Act ... and its implementing regulations."[93] Federal law currently requires that "timely offers" from FPI be considered whenever agencies use "competitive procedures" in procuring products for which FPI has a "significant market share,"[94] and the GAO has found that small business set-asides constitute "competitive procedures" for purposes of this provision.[95] The proposed legislation would effectively overturn this GAO decision as to contracts awarded

---

[89] *See, e.g.*, Steven W. Feldman & Raymond Fioravanti, *Contract Dispute or Bid Protest? The Delex Systems Dilemma*, 39 PUB. CONT. L.J. 483 (2010). *But see* Delex Sys., Inc., B-400403 (Oct. 8, 2008) (determining that task and delivery orders issued under multiple-award ID/IQ contracts are subject to set-asides for small businesses).

[90] P.L. 111-240, §1331, 124 Stat. 2541 (codified at 15 U.S.C. §644(r)).

[91] *Id.* at §1311, 124 Stat. 2537.

[92] In particular, the *Delex* decision, previously noted, did not specifically address the Federal Supply Schedules, and the General Services Administration (GSA) responded to the decision by asserting that Schedules contracts are not subject to set-asides for small businesses because they are governed by a different section of the FAR than other multiple-award contracts. *See* GSA Memorandum from David A. Drabkin, Senior Procurement Executive, to All GSA Contracting Activities, Oct. 28, 2008, quoted in Arnold & Porter LLP, GAO's *Delex* Decision and GSA's Response: The Clash of Titans, *available at* http://www.arnoldporter.com/resources/documents/CA_GAOsDelexDecision&GSAsResponse_012609.pdf (copy on file with the author).

[93] Federal Prison Industries Competition in Contracting Act, H.R. 2098, §2. This legislation would also require that the proportion of the federal market for specific products or services furnished by small businesses during the previous three fiscal years be considered in any proposed expansion of FPI. *Id.* FPI historically enjoyed certain preferences in federal procurement, particularly as to supplies. *See* 18 U.S.C. §4124(a) ("The several Federal departments and agencies and all other Government institutions of the United States shall purchase at not to exceed current market prices, such products of the industries authorized by this chapter as meet their requirements and may be available."). However, several measures enacted since 2001 have sought to limit the degree to which FPI is seen, by some, as "competing" with private-sector firms for the government's business. *See* National Defense Authorization Act for FY2002, P.L. 107-107, §811, 115 Stat. 1180-1181 (Dec. 28, 2001); Bob Stump National Defense Authorization Act for FY2003, P.L. 107-314, §819, 116 Stat. 2612-2613 (Dec. 2, 2002); Intelligence Authorization Act for FY2004, P.L. 108-177, §404, 117 Stat. 2632 (Dec. 13, 2003); Consolidated Appropriations Act, 2004, P.L. 108-199, §637, 118 Stat. 358 (Jan. 23, 2004); Consolidated Appropriations Act, 2005, P.L. 108-447, §637, 118 Stat. 3281 (Dec. 8, 2004); National Defense Authorization Act for FY2008, P.L. 110-181, §827, 122 Stat. 228-229 (Jan. 28, 2008).

[94] 10 U.S.C. §2410n(b)(1) (requirements as to the procurements of defense agencies); P.L. 108-447, §637, 118 Stat. 3281 (imposing similar requirements on the procurements of civilian agencies). The requirements as to civilian agencies are reflected in FAR Subpart 8.6, but are not codified in the United States Code.

[95] Tennier Indus., Inc., B-403946.2 (June 29, 2012). For further discussion of this decision, see CRS Legal Sidebar WSLG177, Federal Prison Industries and Small Businesses: Competing for Federal Procurement Dollars?, by Kate M. Manuel.

---

under the authority of Section 15(a) of the Small Business Act, ensuring that contracts set-aside for small businesses generally (i.e., not of a particular type) cannot be awarded to FPI.[96]

Other measures introduced in the 113th Congress would exempt contracts awarded under the authority of the Small Business Act from restrictions that would be imposed by the proposed legislation.[97]

Small Disadvantaged Businesses Participating in the 8(a) Program

Congress amended Section 8(a) of the Small Business Act in 1978 to authorize agencies to award contracts on a set-aside or sole-source basis to small businesses owned and controlled by socially and economically disadvantaged individuals participating in the SBA's 8(a) Program.[98] Section 8(a) and related provisions of the act broadly define *social disadvantage* and designate certain racial and ethnic groups as socially disadvantaged, although they also grant the SBA authority to recognize additional groups as such.[99] Section 8(a) also defines *economic disadvantage*, but it does not establish any specific monetary thresholds for determining whether individuals are economically disadvantaged.[100] Instead, the SBA promulgated the current "net worth" standards—of not more than $250,000 for initial entry into the program, and $750,000 for continuing eligibility—through notice-and-comment rulemaking in 1989.[101] The act further limits participation in the 8(a) Program to a single term of no more than nine years for firms and individual owners.[102] However, it, along with other provisions of federal law, permits certain

---

[96] The proposed legislation would not appear to bar offers from FPI from being considered for contracts set-aside for various types of small businesses under other provisions of the Small Business Act (i.e., Sections 8(a), 8(m), 31 or 36).

[97] *See* Natural Disaster Fairness in Contracting Act, S. 99, §4(c)(2) (exempting contracts awarded to small businesses from certain restrictions that would be imposed upon the use of noncompetitive awards "in connection with natural disaster reconstruction efforts").

[98] P.L. 85-536, §8(a)(1)-(2), 72 Stat. 384 (codified, as amended, at 15 U.S.C. §637(a)).

[99] *See* 15 U.S.C. §637(a)(5) ("Socially disadvantaged individuals are those who have been subjected to racial or ethnic prejudice or cultural bias because of their identity as a member of a group without regard to their individual qualities."); 15 U.S.C. §631(f)(1)(B)-(C) ("[W]ith respect to the Administration's business development programs the Congress finds that many ... persons are socially disadvantaged because of their identification as members of certain groups that have suffered the effects of discriminatory practices ...; [and] that such groups include, but are not limited to, Black Americans, Hispanic Americans, Native Americans, Indian tribes, Asian Pacific Americans, Native Hawaiian Organizations, and other minorities."); 13 C.F.R. §124.103(d)(4) (procedures for petitioning for recognition as a socially disadvantaged group). Individuals who are not members of groups presumed to be disadvantaged for purposes of the 8(a) Program can seek recognition of "individual social disadvantage." *See* 13 C.F.R. §124.103(c).

[100] *See* 15 U.S.C. §637(a)(5) ("Economically disadvantaged individuals are those socially disadvantaged individuals whose ability to compete in the free enterprise system has been impaired due to diminished capital and credit opportunities as compared to others in the same business area who are not socially disadvantaged.").

[101] *See* Small Bus. Admin., Minority Small Business and Capital Ownership Development Program: Final Rule, 54 Fed. Reg. 34692 (Aug. 21, 1989) (codified, as amended, at 13 C.F.R. §124.104(c)). Individuals' ownership interests in the small business and equity in their primary personal residence are excluded when determining net worth. The SBA's net worth standards are not acquisition-related thresholds subject to periodic adjustment for inflation under Section 807 of the Ronald W. Reagan National Defense Authorization Act for FY2005. *See, e.g.*, Dep't of Defense, Gen. Servs. Admin., & Nat'l Aeronautics & Space Admin., Inflation Adjustment of Acquisition-Related Thresholds, 75 Fed. Reg. 5716, 5717 (Feb. 4, 2010). However, the Department of Transportation adjusted the net worth standards for its Disadvantaged Business Enterprise (DBE) program—which had previously corresponded to SBA's standards—by regulation in 2011, without an express statutory requirement or authorization to do so. Dep't of Transportation, Disadvantaged Business Enterprise Program: Program Improvements, 76 Fed. Reg. 5083, 5085-5086 (Jan. 28, 2011) (codified at 49 C.F.R. §26.27(a)(2)(i)) (increasing the net worth threshold from $750,000 to $1.32 million).

[102] 15 U.S.C. §636(j)(10)(C)(i) (nine-year term); 15 U.S.C. §637(a)(9) (termination and early graduation); 13 C.F.R. (continued...)

---

owner-groups—namely, Alaska Native Corporations (ANCs), Community Development Corporations (CDCs), Indian tribes, and Native Hawaiian Organizations (NHOs)—to participate in the 8(a) Program on somewhat different terms than individual owners.[103] No significant amendments to Section 8(a) have been enacted in recent years, despite the introduction of multiple bills on the topic.[104]

Members of the 113th Congress have also proposed several amendments to Section 8(a). Some bills would increase the SBA's "net worth" standard to $1.5 million for initial and continuing eligibility, and codify this standard.[105] These measures would also permit firms to participate in the 8(a) Program for more than nine years if they have not "completed" a contract awarded under the authority of Section 8(a).[106] These changes would apparently respond to concerns that the current net-worth thresholds are too low and have not been adjusted for inflation.[107] There have also been concerns that the percentage of contract dollars awarded to individual 8(a) firms has decreased as the number of firms participating in the program has increased.[108]

Another measure would amend Section 8(a) to provide that, if an NHO establishes it is economically disadvantaged in connection with the application to the 8(a) Program of one firm it owns, it generally need not reestablish economic disadvantage when additional firms it owns apply to the program.[109] Currently, Section 8(a) has two separate provisions regarding determinations of economic disadvantage, one addressing tribally owned firms, and the other addressing all other firms.[110] Based, in part, on these provisions, the SBA has promulgated regulations which provide that Indian tribes generally need only demonstrate economic disadvantage one time to qualify firms for the 8(a) Program.[111] In contrast, the regulations as to NHO-owned firms provide that:

> For the first 8(a) applicant owned by a particular NHO, individual NHO members must meet the same initial eligibility economic disadvantage thresholds as individually-owned 8(a)

(...continued)

§124.301 (exiting the program); 13 C.F.R. §124.302 (early graduation); 13 C.F.R. §124.303 (termination).

[103] For further discussion, see CRS Report R40744, *The "8(a) Program" for Small Businesses Owned and Controlled by the Socially and Economically Disadvantaged: Legal Requirements and Issues*, by Kate M. Manuel.

[104] *See generally* CRS Report R42390, *Federal Contracting and Subcontracting with Small Businesses: Issues in the 112th Congress*, by Kate M. Manuel and Erika K. Lunder.

[105] *See, e.g.*, Minority Small Business Enhancement Act, H.R. 2550, §2; Expanding Opportunities for Main Street Act, H.R. 2551, §102.

[106] *Id.*

[107] *See, e.g.*, Not Too Small to Succeed in Business Act, H.R. 3754, 112th Cong., §2 (finding that the 8(a) Program does not adequately prepare firms for graduation, in part, because of the "reliance of the [SBA] on outdated measures of ... net worth in determining whether a company participating in the program [is] economically disadvantaged").

[108] *See, e.g.*, Mark Rockwell, *Some Small Firms Doubt Efficacy of SBA Assistance*, FED. COMPUTER WEEK, Feb. 3, 2014, *available at* http://fcw.com/articles/2014/02/03/small-biz-contracting-assistance.aspx.

[109] Native Small Business Conformity Act, S. 1607, §2(b). This amendment would be effective upon its enactment, and would apply to determinations of economic disadvantage made before, on, or after its enactment. The proposed legislation would also amend Section 3(p) of the Small Business Act to include NHO-owned firms within the act's definition of *HUBZone small business concern*. *Id. See infra* note 130 and accompanying text.

[110] *Compare* 15 U.S.C. §637(a)(6)(A) (tribally owned firms) *with* 15 U.S.C. §637(a)(6)(B) (other firms).

[111] *See* 15 U.S.C. §637(a)(6)(A)-(B); 13 C.F.R. §124.109(b) ("Once an Indian Tribe establishes that it is economically disadvantaged in connection with the application for one Tribally-owned firm, it need not reestablish such status in order to have other businesses that it owns certified for 8(a) ... program participation, unless specifically requested to do so by [SBA officials].").

---

applicants [i.e., $250,000]. For any additional 8(a) applicant owned by the NHO, individual NHO members must meet the economic disadvantage thresholds for continued 8(a) eligibility [i.e., $750,000].[112]

By providing that NHOs generally need only establish economic disadvantage one time, the proposed legislation would effectively require that the SBA treat NHO-owned firms in the same way it currently treats tribally owned firms.

Women-Owned Small Businesses

Congress added Section 8(m) to the Small Business Act in 2000 in order to authorize set-asides for women-owned small businesses.[113] The SBA has construed Section 8(m) as authorizing agencies to set aside contracts for women-owned small businesses in industries where such firms are "substantially underrepresented," and for economically disadvantaged women-owned small businesses in industries where such firms are "underrepresented."[114] However, due in part to difficulties in determining the industries in which women-owned small businesses are underrepresented, set-asides for women-owned small businesses were not actually implemented until 2011.[115] Nonetheless, despite its relatively recent implementation, Section 8(m) has already been subject to one significant amendment. Namely, the 112th Congress removed caps on the maximum value of contracts that could be set aside for women-owned small businesses,[116] thereby making set-asides for women-owned small businesses more like those for other types of small businesses (e.g., HUBZone, service-disabled veteran-owned), as illustrated in **Table 1**. As

---

[112] 13 C.F.R. §124.110(c)(1).

[113] Small Business Reauthorization Act of 2000, P.L. 106-554, tit. VIII, §811, 114 Stat. 2763A-708 (Dec. 21, 2000) (codified, as amended, at 15 U.S.C. §637(m)).

[114] 15 U.S.C. §637(a)(6)(A). Women are generally considered to be economically disadvantaged if their personal net worth is less than $750,000 (excluding their ownership interest in the business and equity interest in their primary personal residence). 13 C.F.R. §127.203(b)(1).

[115] Implementation was initially delayed by the requirement that set-asides be limited to industries in which women are underrepresented or substantially underrepresented. The SBA's first proposed rule regarding eligible industries identified only four (i.e., intelligence; engraving and metalworking; furniture and kitchen cabinet manufacturing; and motor vehicle dealerships). U.S. Small Bus. Admin., Proposed Rule: Women-Owned Small Business Federal Contract Assistance Procedures, 72 Fed. Reg. 73285 (Dec. 27, 2007). This proposed rule was widely criticized, including by some Members of Congress, and the SBA revised it to include an additional 27 industries. *See, e.g., Sens. Snowe, Dole Offer Bill to Overhaul Rule on Women-Owned Small Business Set Asides*, 89 FED. CONT. REP. 180 (Feb. 19, 2008); Robert Brodsky, *SBA Issues New Proposal on Small Business Program, But Same Questions Remain*, GOV'T EXEC., Sept. 30, 2008, *available at* http://www.govexec.com/dailyfed/0908/093008rb1 htm. However, before the revised rule could be finalized, the U.S. Court of Appeals for the Federal Circuit issued its decision in *Rothe Development Corporation v. Department of Defense*, striking down a race-conscious contracting program on the grounds that there was insufficient evidence of discrimination in the defense industry before Congress when it created the program. 545 F.3d 1023 (Fed. Cir. 2008). Although gender-conscious programs are subject to "intermediate scrutiny," not "strict scrutiny" like the race-conscious program at issue in *Rothe*, the SBA extended the comment period on the proposed rule in order to "review[]" how its determinations regarding the industries in which women are underrepresented might fare under *Rothe's* standard for a "strong basis in evidence." U.S. Small Bus. Admin., The Women-Owned Small Business Federal Contracting Assistance Procedures: Eligible Industries, 74 Fed. Reg. 1153 (Jan. 12, 2009). Then, in March 2009, Congress enacted the Omnibus Appropriations Act, 2009, which temporarily prohibited implementation of the proposed rule. P.L. 111-8, Administrative Provisions—Small Business Administration, §522, 123 Stat. 673 (Mar. 11, 2009). Subsequently, however, the Obama Administration finalized regulations identifying 83 industries in which women are underrepresented or substantially underrepresented, and these regulations took effect on February 4, 2011. U.S. Small Bus. Admin., Women-Owned Small Business Federal Contract Program: Final Rule, 75 Fed. Reg. 62258 (Oct. 7, 2010).

[116] P.L. 112-239, at §1697, 126 Stat. 2091.

---

initially enacted, Section 8(m) only permitted set-asides of contracts whose value was below $3 million, or $5 million for manufacturing contracts (later adjusted to $4 million ($6.5 million for manufacturing contracts)).[117] However, legislation enacted by the 112th Congress removed these caps, permitting "larger" contracts to be set aside for women-owned small businesses.

Measures introduced in the 113th Congress would go a step further by authorizing agencies to award sole-source contracts valued at up to $4 million ($6.5 million for manufacturing contracts) to women-owned small businesses.[118] Such legislation would, if enacted, permit sole-source awards to women-owned small businesses like those permitted to other types of small businesses. See **Table 1**. Several commentators have suggested that such an amendment is necessary for women-owned small businesses to be treated similarly to other types of small businesses.[119] However, authorizations of "sole source" awards have historically proved controversial because of the values associated with competition in federal contracting.[120]

HUBZone Small Businesses

Congress added Section 31 to the Small Business Act in 1997 to permit agencies to set aside contracts for HUBZone small businesses, make sole-source awards to such firms, and grant them "price evaluation adjustments" in unrestricted competitions.[121] To be eligible for these preferences, firms must meet certain criteria, which include having their principal office in a HUBZone.[122] At least 35% of their employees must also reside in a HUBZone.[123] Section 3 of the Small Business Act, in turn, defines a *HUBZone* to include "qualified census tracts" and "qualified nonmetropolitan counties," the latter of which includes counties in which "the median household income is less than 80 percent of the nonmetropolitan State median income, based on the most recent data available from the Bureau of the Census," among other things.[124] Also included within the definition of *HUBZone* are "redesignated areas," or areas that ceased to qualify as census tracts or nonmetropolitan counties, but were allowed to remain HUBZones until the later of (1) the date on which the Census Bureau publicly released the first results from the

---

[117] *See* 15 U.S.C. §637(m)(2)(D) (2010).

[118] Women's Procurement Program Equalization Act, H.R. 2452, §2. House Rules Committee Amendment No. 183, to H.R. 4435, as passed by the House, House of Representatives Committee on Rules, H.R. 4435, *available at* http://rules house.gov/bill/113/hr-4435; House Armed Services Committee, FY15-H.R. 4435 Floor Amendments and Tracker, *available at* http://armedservices house.gov/index.cfm?p=fy15-h-r-4435-floor-amendments-and-tracker.

[119] *See, e.g.,* Jon Williams and Megan Connor, *Setting Aside the Glass Ceiling: The Women-Owned Small Business Program Should Have the Same Advantages as the Other Set-Aside Programs,* 101 FED. CONTR. REP. 367 (Apr. 1, 2014); Lillian F. McManus, *The Anatomy of a Helping Hand: Women-Owned Small Businesses and Federal Contract Procurement,* 18 WM. & MARY J. WOMEN & L. 625 (2012).

[120] *See supra* note 81 and accompanying text.

[121] Small Business Reauthorization Act of 1997, P.L. 105-135, tit. VI, §602(b)(1)(B), 111 Stat. 2629 (Dec. 2, 1997) (codified, as amended, at 15 U.S.C. §657a) For purposes of Section 31, a price evaluation adjustment entails adding up to 10% to the price of all offers except (1) offers from HUBZone small businesses that have not waived the evaluation preference and (2) otherwise successful offers from small businesses, when determining which offer has the lowest price or represents the "best value" for the government. *See* 48 C.F.R. §52.219-4(b)(i)-(ii).

[122] 15 U.S.C. §632(p)(5)(A)(I)(aa).

[123] *Id.*

[124] *See generally* 15 U.S.C. §632(p)(4).

2010 decennial census, or (2) three years after the date on which the census tract or nonmetropolitan county ceased to qualify.[125]

Section 31 and the provisions of Section 3 pertaining to HUBZones have been periodically amended over the years, often in response to the release of decennial census data. Release of 2010 census data, in particular, affected the grounds upon which a number of firms qualified as HUBZone small businesses,[126] and prompted the 112th Congress to enact legislation permitting certain "base closure areas" (i.e., military bases that have been closed) to continue to be treated as HUBZones for an additional period.[127] Specifically, this legislation permits areas that were treated as HUBZones pursuant to Section 152(a)(2) of the Small Business Reauthorization and Manufacturing Assistance Act of 2004 to be treated as HUBZones for up to five years, provided that no area may be treated as a HUBZone for more than five years under the authority of this legislation and/or the 2004 act. Section 152(a)(2), in turn, provided for "base closure areas" that had undergone final closure to be treated as HUBZones for five years, and defined *base closure area* to include military installations closed pursuant to the Defense Base Closure and Realignment Act of 1990 and other authorities.[128]

Similar legislation has been introduced in the 113th Congress to amend the definition of *base closure area* so that it includes the municipalities, counties, and census tracts where the military base was located that have a total population of not more than 50,000.[129] Census tracts that are "contiguous" to such census tracts would also be included.

Other legislation introduced in the 113th Congress would amend the definition of *HUBZone small business concern* in Section 3(p) of the Small Business Act to include small businesses owned and controlled by NHOs.[130] Currently, small businesses owned and controlled by ANCs, Indian tribes, and CDCs are among those listed here, but small businesses owned and controlled by NHOs are not. ANCs, CDCs, Indian tribes, and NHOs are generally (although not universally) treated the same for purposes of other provisions of federal procurement law,[131] which would appear to be the rationale for including NHO's in Section 3(p)'s definition of *HUBZone small business concern.*

Service-Disabled Veteran-Owned Small Businesses

Congress added Section 36 to the Small Business Act in 2003 to permit agencies to set aside contracts for service-disabled veteran-owned small businesses, and to make sole-source awards of contracts valued at up to $3.5 million ($6 million for manufacturing contracts) to such firms.[132] Section 36 has not been substantively amended since then. However, Congress enacted additional

---

[125] 15 U.S.C. §632(p)(4)(C)(i)-(ii).

[126] *See generally* CRS Report R41268, *Small Business Administration HUBZone Program*, by Robert Jay Dilger.

[127] P.L. 112-239, §1698, 126 Stat. 2091-2092.

[128] *See* Consolidated Appropriations Act, 2005, P.L. 108-447, §152, 118 Stat. 3456-3457 (Dec. 8, 2004).

[129] HUBZone Expansion Act, H.R. 489, §2; & S. 206, §2.

[130] *See* Native Small Business Conformity Act, S. 1607, §2(a)(1).

[131] *See generally* CRS Report R40744, *The "8(a) Program" for Small Businesses Owned and Controlled by the Socially and Economically Disadvantaged: Legal Requirements and Issues,* by Kate M. Manuel.

[132] Veterans Benefits Act of 2003, P.L. 108-183, tit. III, §308, 117 Stat. 2662 (Dec. 16, 2003) (codified, as amended, in 15 U.S.C. §657f).

legislation pertaining to set-asides and sole-source awards by the Department of Veterans Affairs to service-disabled veteran-owned small businesses and other veteran-owned small businesses in 2006.[133] The latter authority is part of the Veterans Benefits Act; it is separate and distinct from the authority provided under the Small Business Act.[134] There is some overlap between the programs under these two acts, in that the Small Business Act relies upon the definitions of *veteran* and *service-disabled veteran* given in the Veterans Benefits Act.[135] However, there are also a number of differences between the two programs. Perhaps most notably, firms and their owners must have their eligibility verified by the VA to be eligible for contracting preferences under the Veterans Benefits Act, while they may "self-certify" as to their eligibility for preferences under the Small Business Act.[136] In addition, the Veterans Benefits Act permits firms owned by the surviving spouses of certain veterans to participate in the program for up to 10 years, while the Small Business Act does not.[137]

The existence of two separate set-aside programs—under different statutory authorities and with different rules—benefitting broadly the same population has prompted some concern and confusion.[138] Legislation introduced in the 113th Congress would respond to this situation by standardizing eligibility requirements for the two programs.[139] Specifically, this legislation would amend the Small Business Act so that it corresponds to the Veterans Benefits Act (1) in its definition of *service-disabled veteran-owned small business*, and (2) in permitting certain surviving spouses of veterans to participate in the program for a period of time. Currently, businesses that are majority owned by one or more veterans with service-connected disabilities that "are permanent and total" who are unable to manage the daily business operations are included within the definition of *service-disabled veteran-owned small business* under the Veterans Benefits Act, but not under the Small Business Act.[140] Similarly, certain surviving spouses of veterans may continue participating in the program for a period of time after the veteran's death under the Veterans Benefits Act, but not the Small Business Act.[141] The proposed legislation would amend the Small Business Act so that its treatment of both these issues corresponds to that in the Veterans Benefits Act. At least one proposed bill would also require that

---

[133] Veterans Benefits, Health Care, and Information Technology Act of 2006, P.L. 109-461, 120 Stat. 3431 (Dec. 22, 2006) (codified, as amended, in part, at 38 U.S.C. §§8127-8128).

[134] *See* VA's "Veterans First" Contracting Program, below.

[135] *See* 15 U.S.C. §632(q)(1) & (4).

[136] *Compare* 38 U.S.C. §8127(e) ("A small business concern may be awarded a contract under this section only if the small business concern and the veteran owner of the small business concern are listed in the database of veteran-owned businesses maintained by the Secretary.") *with* 13 C.F.R. §125.15(a) (permitting firms to "represent" that they are service-disabled veteran-owned small businesses as part of their bid or offer).

[137] *Compare* 38 U.S.C. §8127(h) *with* 13 C.F.R. Part 125, Subparts A-E.

[138] *See, e.g.*, Nichole A. Best, *Safeguarding Opportunities for America's Wounded Warriors: A Proposed Solution to Subcontracting Abuse in the Service-Disabled Veteran-Owned Small Business Program and the Veterans First Contracting Program*, 42 PUB. CONT. L.J. 347 (2013).

[139] *See, e.g.*, Improving Opportunities for Service-Disabled Veteran-Owned Small Businesses Act, H.R. 2882 & S. 2334; National Defense Authorization Act for FY2015, H.R. 4435, as reported in the House, §812(a).

[140] *Compare* H.R. 2882, §2; S. 2334, §2; *and* H.R. 4435, as reported in the House, §812(a) *with* 38 U.S.C. §8127(*l*)(2). The proposed legislation would also delete the text defining *small business concern owned and controlled by veterans* from the Veterans Benefits Act, and instead incorporate by reference the Small Business Act's definition of this term.

[141] H.R. 2882, at §2; S. 2334, §2; H.R. 4435, as reported in the House, §812(a). As is currently the case under the Veterans Benefits Act, the proposed provisions of the Small Business Act would apply only to the surviving spouses of veterans with service-connected disabilities rated as 100% disabling, or who die as a result of the service-connected disability. *Compare* 38 U.S.C. §8127(h) *with* H.R. 2882, at §2; S. 2334, §2; *and* H.R. 4435, as reported in the House, §812(a).

---

service-disabled veteran-owned small businesses have their eligibility, and that of their owners, verified in order to them to be eligible for awards under the Small Business Act, as is currently required under the Veterans Benefits Act.[142] Other bills would not.[143]

The proposed legislation would also require the SBA and the VA to enter into an agreement whereby the SBA would take over "control and administration" of VA's "Veterans First" contracting program, discussed below.[144] The legislation would not, however, appear to completely merge the two programs, since it would not amend the provisions in Section 36 of the Small Business Act that authorize agencies other than the VA to make set-aside and sole-source awards to service-disabled veteran-owned small businesses. Other agencies would, for example, continue to lack authority to make set-aside and sole-source awards to small businesses owned by veterans who are not service-disabled. They would also not be required to set aside contracts for veteran-owned businesses, as the VA has generally been found to be under the Veterans Benefits Act.[145] In addition, the Small Business Act would only permit sole-source awards of contracts that do not involve manufacturing whose value is at or below $3.5 million, while the Veterans Benefits Act would permit sole-source awards of contracts that do not involve manufacturing whose value is at or below $5 million.[146]

Creation of Additional Set-Aside Programs

As previously noted, there are currently set-aside programs for HUBZone small businesses, women-owned small businesses, service-disabled veteran-owned small businesses, certain small disadvantaged businesses,[147] and small businesses not belonging to any of the foregoing types under the authority of the Small Business Act. The most recent of these programs were not created until 2003, in the case of the program for service-disabled veteran-owned small businesses, and not implemented until 2011, in the case of the program for women-owned small businesses. However, some have called for the establishment of additional set-aside programs that would benefit certain small businesses and, potentially, others. At least one measure introduced in

---

[142] H.R. 4435, as reported in the House, §812(a) (including, in the amended definition of *small business concern owned and controlled by service-disabled veterans* within the Small Business Act, the requirement that the business be listed in the "database described in section 8127(f) of title 38, United States Code").

[143] H.R. 2882, at §2 (including no requirement for inclusion in the VA's database); S. 2334, §2 (same).

[144] H.R. 2882, at §4; H.R. 4435, as reported in the House, §812(b). S. 2334 does not include this requirement. It would, however, require a GAO study of whether it is practicable for either the SBA or the VA to have "[g]overnment-wide responsibility" for verifying the status of veteran-owned small businesses.

[145] *See infra* note 194 and accompanying text.

[146] *Compare* 48 C.F.R. §19.1406(a)(1) ("A contracting officer shall consider a contract award to a [service-disabled veteran-owned] concern on a sole source basis ... provided ... [t]he anticipated award price of the contract, including options, will not exceed (i) $6 million for a requirement within the NAICS codes for manufacturing; or (ii) $3.5 million for a requirement within any other NAICS code") *with* 48 C.F.R. §819.7007(a)(1) ("A contracting officer may award contracts to [service-disabled veteran-owned concerns on a sole source basis provided ... [t]he anticipated award price of the contract (including options) will not exceed $5 million," among other things); 48 C.F.R. §819.7008(a)(1) (similar, as to other veteran-owned small businesses).

[147] Small disadvantaged businesses and individual owners may only participate in the 8(a) Program one time, for a maximum of nine years. *See* 15 U.S.C. §636(j)(10)(C)(i) (nine-year term); 15 U.S.C. §637(a)(9) (termination and early graduation); 13 C.F.R. §124.301 (exiting the 8(a) Program); 13 C.F.R. §124.302 (early graduation); 13 C.F.R. §124.303 (termination from the Program). This limitation would appear to be one reason that some Members of Congress have supported the creation of additional set-aside programs that could benefit small disadvantaged businesses and owners who have completed their 8(a) Program term.

---

the 113th Congress would, for example, authorize a set-aside program for businesses "owned or controlled by historically disadvantaged individuals," a category which would be defined by reference to the Department of Commerce's Minority Business Development Agency's (MBDA's) definition of *socially or economically disadvantaged groups*.[148] Small businesses meeting specified criteria (e.g., owners' net worth no greater than $2 million; principal place of business in the United States) would be eligible for set-asides through this program. However, eligibility would not be limited to small businesses, as it would have been under similar measures introduced in the 112th Congress.[149]

Surety Bond Guarantees

Various provisions of federal law require government contractors—including small businesses—to post performance and payment bonds.[150] These and other types of bonds may also be required in conjunction with state, local, and private contracts. However, small businesses have historically had difficulty posting such bonds because of their limited access to capital.[151] Thus, Congress amended Section 411 of the Small Business Investment Act in 1970 to authorize the SBA to guarantee certain bonds posted by small businesses that cannot obtain bonding on "reasonable terms and conditions" through regular commercial channels without the SBA's guarantee.

Initially, Section 411 only permitted the SBA to guarantee bonds for contracts valued at $500,000 or less.[152] However, Congress has increased the maximum contract value over the years, including to $2 million in 2000.[153] The recession of 2007-2009 prompted a further increase, to $5 million ($10 million if the contracting officer certified that a larger guarantee is "necessary"),[154]

---

[148] Expanding Opportunities for Main Street Act, H.R. 2551, §205. Because the MBDA's definition includes "Hasidic Jews," basing eligibility for set-aside contracts on the MBDA's definition could potentially raise First Amendment issues insofar as "Hasidic Jews" is viewed as a religious classification, rather than a cultural one. *Cf.* Bd. of Ed. of Kiryas Joel Village School Dist. v. Grumet, 512 U.S. 687, 741 (1994) (Scalia, J., dissenting) (suggesting that the New York law in question, which resulted in a village that was a religious enclave being carved out as a separate school district, could be seen as reflecting cultural, rather than religious, groupings).

[149] *See, e.g.*, Early Stage Small Business Contracting Act of 2012, 112th Cong., H.R. 4121 (requiring agencies to award contracts whose value is between $3,000 and "less than half the upper threshold of Section 15(j)(1) of the Small Business Act" to *early stage small business concerns*, or firms with fewer than 15 employees that have average annual receipts of not more than $1 million (unless the concern is in an industry with an average annual revenue standard of less than $1 million)); National Defense Authorization Act for FY2013, H.R. 4310, as passed by the House, at §1693a, 112th Cong. (same).

[150] *See* 40 U.S.C. §3131(b)(1)-(2) (generally requiring the posting of performance and payment bonds on contracts of more than $150,000 for the construction, alteration, or repair of a "public building or public work of the Federal government"). Agencies may also require bid bonds in certain circumstances. *See* 48 C.F.R. §28.101-1. Performance bonds assure the government that the work under the contract will be completed. Payment bonds ensure subcontractors and materialmen under the contract that they will be able to obtain payment. Bid bonds ensure that the contractor will enter into a contract based on the terms of its bid or offer. A bond is a promise by a surety, or third party, to pay any debts of the contractor or make good any default by or failure of the contractor to satisfy a contractual obligation. *See* Taylor Constr. Inc. v. ABT Serv. Corp., Inc., 163 F.3d 1119 (9th Cir. 1998).

[151] *See generally* CRS Report R42037, *SBA Surety Bond Guarantee Program*, by Robert Jay Dilger.

[152] Housing and Urban Development Act of 1970, P.L. 91-609, tit. IX, §911(a)(4), 84 Stat. 1813-1814 (Dec. 31, 1970).

[153] Consolidated Appropriations Act, 2001, P.L. 106-554, tit. VIII, §805(a), 114 Stat. 2763A–705 (Dec. 21, 2000) (codified, as amended, at 15 U.S.C. §694b(a)(1)(A)).

[154] *See, e.g.,* 155 CONG. REC. S1486 (daily ed., Feb. 4, 2009) (statement by Sen. Snowe) (temporarily increasing the bond limit is necessary to "ensure that small businesses are able to secure the surety bonds they need to compete for (continued...)

---

although this increase was a temporary one, lasting only from February 17, 2009, through September 30, 2010.[155] Subsequently, though, the 112th Congress increased the maximum contract value to $6.5 million, and provided for the cap to be adjusted for inflation every five years pursuant to Section 807 of the Ronald W. Reagan National Defense Authorization Act for FY2005.[156]

Legislation introduced in the 113th Congress would build on these changes by increasing the maximum percentage of the surety's loss that the SBA may pay in the event of a default by the contractor. Section 411 currently provides for a maximum guarantee of 70%, in the case of sureties authorized to issue bonds subject to the SBA's guarantee (90% in the case of sureties requiring the SBA's specific approval for the issuance of a bond).[157] However, bills introduced in the 113th Congress would amend Section 411 to permit the SBA to pay up to 90% of losses paid by sureties authorized to issue bonds subject to the SBA's guarantee, regardless of whether the SBA had to specifically approve the issuance of the bond.[158] The maximum guarantee would remain 90% for sureties requiring the SBA's "specific approval" for the issuance of a bond.

Reverse Auctions

The term *reverse auction* generally connotes a bidding procedure wherein sellers compete to determine who is willing to offer their supplies or services at the lowest price. Federal law does not expressly authorize—or directly regulate—the use of reverse auctions by federal agencies. However, the GAO has found that the use of reverse auctions is permissible pursuant to FAR provisions that authorize the use of procurement practices and procedures that are not "prohibited by law."[159] The use of reverse auctions by federal agencies has reportedly increased recently,[160]

(...continued)

contracts, grow, and hire more employees," and "in our current economic recession, small businesses are finding it even more difficult to secure the credit lines necessary to get bonds in the private sector"); 155 CONG. REC. S2283 (daily ed., Feb. 13, 2009) (statement by Sen. Cardin) (similar).

[155] American Recovery and Reinvestment Act, P.L. 111-5, §508, 123 Stat. 158-159 (Feb. 17, 2009). ARRA also temporarily modified the size standards for the SBA's surety bond guarantee program so that businesses were eligible for the program if they (and their affiliates) did not exceed the size standard for the primary industry in which the business was engaged. *Id.* This change allowed more businesses to qualify for the program, and the SBA subsequently adopted regulations that extended this change to post-ARRA guarantees. *See* Small Bus. Admin., Surety Bond Guarantee Program; Size Standards: Direct Final Rule, 76 Fed. Reg. 48549, 48550 (Aug. 11, 2010) (codified at 13 C.F.R. §121.301(d)(2)). The 112th Congress later enacted legislation that essentially codified this SBA regulation. *See* P.L. 112-239, §1695(c), 126 Stat. 2090.

[156] P.L. 112-239, §1695(a), 126 Stat. 2089-2090.

[157] 15 U.S.C. §694b(c)(1)-(2).

[158] *See* Security in Bonding Act, H.R. 776, §3; National Defense Authorization Act for FY2015, H.R. 4435, as reported in the House, §818. A similar provision was included in an amendment (Amendment 2, as numbered by the House Rules Committee) to the House-passed National Defense Authorization Act for FY2015. However, this amendment also addresses pledges of assets by sureties and requires GAO to study agency practices as to surety bonds). *See* House of Representatives Committee on Rules, H.R. 4435, *available at* http://rules.house.gov/bill/113/hr-4435; House Armed Services Committee, FY15-H.R. 4435 Floor Amendments and Tracker, *available at* http://armedservices.house.gov/index.cfm?p=fy15-h-r-4435-floor-amendments-and-tracker.

[159] *See* MTB Group, Inc., B-295463 (Feb. 23, 2005) (quoting 48 C.F.R. §1.102(d)).

[160] Gov't Accountability Office, Reverse Auctions: Guidance Is Needed to Maximize Competition and Achieve Cost Savings, GAO-14-200T, Dec. 11, 2013 (reporting that the use of reverse auctions by the four agencies sampled—the Departments of the Army, Homeland Security, the Interior, and Veterans Affairs—increased by almost 175% between FY2008 and FY2012).

---

prompting some concern that such auctions could be detrimental to small businesses, which are generally less able to compete on price than larger firms.[161]

Legislation introduced in the 113th Congress would respond to these concerns, as well as related concerns that agencies may use reverse auctions in inappropriate circumstances (e.g., with supplies or services that cannot be evaluated strictly on price).[162] The legislation in the 113th Congress would add a new section to the Small Business Act prohibiting the use of "reverse auction methods" for certain contracts "suitable" for award to a small business, or that are to be awarded pursuant to those sections of the Small Business Act that require or permit set-asides and sole-source awards to small businesses (i.e., Sections 8(a), 8(m), 15(a), 15(j), 31 and 36).[163] One bill would prohibit the use of reverse auctions only with contracts for *design and construction services*, which the bill would define to include site planning and landscaping design; architectural and interior design; engineering system design; delivery and supply of construction materials; and construction, alteration, or repair.[164] Another bill would prohibit the use of reverse auctions with any contract for "services, including design and construction services," as well as with contracts for supplies in which the offeror's technical qualifications constitute "part of the basis" for the award.[165] The latter bill would also extend these limitations to the use of reverse auctions to contracts awarded to service-disabled veteran-owned small businesses and other veteran-owned small businesses by the VA under the authority of the Veterans Benefits Act. The former would not.[166]

Design-Build Contracts

Section 4105 of the Federal Acquisition Reform Act (FARA) of 1996 generally requires agencies to use "two-phase selection procedures" when contracting for the design and construction of public buildings or works, provided certain conditions are met.[167] In the first phase, the agency solicits information about offerors' technical approaches and qualifications, without considering cost or price.[168] Based on these submissions, the agency then selects the "most highly qualified"

---

[161] *See, e.g.,* Mark Rockwell, *Experts Debate the Value of Reverse Auctions,* FED. COMPUTER WEEK, Dec. 11, 2013, *available at* http://fcw.com/articles/2013/12/11/experts-debate-value-of-reverse-auctions.aspx.

[162] *See, e.g.,* Jill R. Aitoro, *Contractors: Reverse Auctions Favor Low Cost Over Best Value,* WASH. BUS. J., Jan. 28, 2011, *available at* http://www.bizjournals.com/washington/print-edition/2011/01/28/contractors-reverse-auctions-favor html?page=all.

[163] *See* Commonsense Construction Contracting Act, H.R. 2751, §2; National Defense Authorization Act for FY2015, as reported in the House, H.R. 4435, §815.

[164] The proposed legislation's definition of *reverse auction* would encompass "real-time auction[s] on the Internet between a group of offerors who compete ... by submitting bids for a contract or task order with the ability to submit revised bids throughout the course of the auction, and the award being made to the offeror who submits the lowest bid." H.R. 2751, §2.

[165] H.R. 4435, §815. This measure's definition of *reverse auction* is broader than that in H.R. 2751. It would include any "real-time auction conducted through an electronic medium between a group of offerors who compete against each other by submitting offers for a contract or task order with the ability to submit revised offers throughout the course of the auction."

[166] *Compare* H.R. 2751, §2 *with* H.R. 4435, §815.

[167] P.L. 104–106, div. D, tit. XLI, §4105(b)(1), 110 Stat. 647 (Feb. 10, 1996) (codified, as amended, at 41 U.S.C. §3309). These conditions include, but are not limited to, the following: (1) three or more offers are anticipated; (2) the design work must be performed before the offeror can develop a cost or price proposal; and (3) the offeror will incur substantial expenses in preparing the offer. *See* 41 U.S.C. §3309(b)(1)-(4).

[168] 41 U.S.C. §3309(c)(1)-(3).

offerors from the first phase and invites them to submit proposals for a second phase of the competition that considers cost or price, among other things.[169] Section 4105 further provides that the first-phase solicitation must state the maximum number of offerors who will be selected for consideration in the second phase, and that this number cannot exceed five unless the contracting agency determines, on a case-by-case basis, that a "specified number greater than 5 is in the Federal Government's interest and is consistent with the purposes and objectives of the two-phase selection process."[170] However, concerns have been raised that agencies select more than five offerors in too many cases, thereby imposing the costs of competing on firms—particularly small businesses—that are progressively less likely to be selected as the number of competitors increases.[171]

At least one measure introduced in the 113th Congress would respond to these concerns by amending the codification of Section 4105 (i.e., 41 U.S.C. §3309) to require that (1) contracting officers document how selecting more than five firms is consistent with the purposes of the two-phase selection process, and (2) agency heads approve these justifications before a procurement contemplating more than five finalists proceeds.[172] Currently, contracting officers must *determine* that selection of more than five firms is consistent with the purposes of the two-phase selection process, but they are not required by statute to *document* this determination in writing. Nor is the approval of the agency head presently required.

The proposed legislation would also generally require the use of two-phase selection procedures in contracts whose value exceeds $750,000, with the apparent intent of foreclosing the use with such contracts of design-bid-build or other procedures expressly authorized by statute.[173] Agencies would also be required to provide public notice of all cases in which they select more than five finalists, or do not use two-phase selection procedures with contracts valued in excess of $750,000.[174] While the amendments that would be made by this legislation do not involve the Small Business Act or expressly refer to small businesses, its drafters have indicated, through the bill's title, that it is intended to benefit small businesses.[175]

"Small" Contracts Reserved for Small Businesses

Federal law currently distinguishes between (1) purchases whose value is below the micro-purchase threshold (generally $3,000);[176] (2) those whose value is above the micro-purchase

---

[169] 41 U.S.C. §3309(c)(4).

[170] 41 U.S.C. §3309(d).

[171] *See, e.g.*, Joseph C. Kovars, Turning a Battleship: Design-Build on Federal Construction Projects, Winter 2011, *available at* http://www.ober.com/publications/1172-turning-battleship-design-build-federal-construction-projects. (noting concerns about the design-build selection process, including concerns specific to small businesses).

[172] *See* Design-Build Efficiency and Jobs Act, H.R. 2750, §2.

[173] *Id.* Currently, Section 4105 permits the use of "the traditional acquisition approach of design-bid-build established under sections 1101 to 1104 of title 40 or another acquisition procedure authorized by law," as well as the two-phase selection procedure it prescribes. 41 U.S.C. §3309(a).

[174] *See* Design-Build Efficiency and Jobs Act, H.R. 2750, §2. In addition, GAO would be required to assess agency compliance with these requirements. *Id.*

[175] The legislation is titled a bill "[t]o amend title 41, United States Code, to require the use of two-phase selection procedures when design-build contracts are suitable for award to small business concerns, and for other purposes."

[176] The micropurchase threshold can be lower or higher than $3,000, depending upon the supplies or services acquired and the circumstances of the acquisition. Micropurchases involving construction services subject to the Davis-Bacon (continued...)

threshold, but below the simplified acquisition threshold (generally $150,000);[177] and (3) other purchases. In particular, Section 15(j) of the Small Business Act and its implementing regulations have long provided that those acquisitions whose value falls between the micro-purchase threshold and the simplified acquisition threshold are "exclusively reserved" for small businesses.[178] However, there have been periodic reports of contracts whose value suggests that they should have been awarded to small businesses going to contractors that do not qualify as "small" under the criteria of the Small Business Act.[179] The 111th Congress responded, in part, to these reports by requiring the OMB, in consultation with the GSA, to issue guidelines regarding one of the most commonly used simplified acquisition methods: government-wide commercial purchase cards.[180] The OMB issued this guidance on December 19, 2011, reminding agencies that those holding government-wide commercial purchase cards should consider small businesses "to the maximum extent practicable" when making micro-purchases.[181]

Notwithstanding the issuance of this guidance, at least one Member of the 113th Congress has introduced legislation that would increase the value of the "small purchases" that are reserved for small businesses.[182] Among other things, this legislation would generally require agencies "to the extent practicable" to award contracts whose value exceeds $3,000, but is below $500,000, to small businesses.[183] The legislation would also grant contracting officers additional authority to award contracts whose value is within this range to small businesses on a sole-source basis.[184] Specifically, it would authorize agencies to make sole-source awards of contracts valued at

---

(...continued)

Act, or other services subject to the Service Contract Act, have lower limits: $2,000 and $2,500, respectively. Those for goods or services that the agency head determines will be used to support contingency operations or facilitate defense against or recovery from nuclear, biological, chemical, or radiological attacks have higher limits: $15,000 in the case of contracts to be awarded or performed inside the United States, and $30,000 in the case of those outside the United States. 48 C.F.R. §13.201(g)(1)(i)-(ii).

[177] In the case of supplies or services to be used in support of contingency operations or to facilitate defense against or recovery from nuclear, biological, chemical, or radiological attacks, the simplified acquisition threshold is $300,000 for contracts awarded and performed inside the United States, and $1 million for contracts awarded and performed outside the United States. 48 C.F.R. §2.101.

[178] 15 U.S.C. §644(j)(1). The regulations implementing Section 15(j) do, however, place certain limitations on the circumstances in which "small purchases" must be exclusively reserved for small businesses. *See* 48 C.F.R. §19.000(b) (excluding contracts awarded and/or performed overseas); 48 C.F.R. §8.404(a) (excluding purchases through the Federal Supply Schedules); 48 C.F.R. §19.502-2(a) (authorizing agencies to solicit small purchases on an unrestricted basis if they receive "no acceptable offers from responsible small businesses").

[179] *See, e.g.*, Danielle Ivory, *Big Firms Edge Out Small for Billions in Awards*, *Bloomberg Gov't*, Nov. 13, 2011 (reporting that "about $4.74 billion, or 45 percent, of more than $10.6 billion targeted for small businesses under government acquisition rules were won by bigger competitors in the year that ended Sept. 30, 2011").

[180] P.L. 111-240, §1332, 124 Stat. 2541.

[181] Exec. Office of the President, Office of Mgmt. & Budget, Increasing Opportunities for Small Businesses in Purchase Card Micro-Purchases, Dec. 19, 2011, *available at* http://www.whitehouse.gov/sites/default/files/omb/procurement/memo/increasing-opportunities-for-small-businesses-in-purchase-card-micro-purchases.pdf. For more on government-wide commercial purchase cards, see generally CRS Report RL34602, *Misuse of Government Purchase Cards*, by Garrett Hatch. Other simplified acquisition procedures include purchase orders, blanket purchase agreements, imprest funds, third-party drafts, and certain standard forms. *See* 48 C.F.R. Subpart 13.3.

[182] *See* Expanding Opportunities for Main Street Act, H.R. 2551, §101.

[183] *Id.* This legislation would also give the SBA additional control over procuring agencies by requiring agencies to notify the SBA of any determinations by such agencies that award of a contract to a small business is not practicable. The legislation would authorize the SBA to open the solicitation for the submission of additional offers, if it determines that doing so is appropriate.

[184] *Id.*

between $150,000 and $500,000 to women-owned small businesses, or other small businesses that are not 8(a), HUBZone, or service-disabled veteran-owned small businesses. The Small Business Act currently does not authorize sole-source awards to firms other than HUBZone small businesses; service-disabled veteran-owned small businesses; and small disadvantaged businesses participating in the 8(a) Program. Rather, it only authorizes agencies to set aside contracts for other small businesses, as **Table 1** illustrates.

Definition of "Small Business"

Section 3 of the Small Business Act currently prescribes criteria that entities must meet to qualify as "small businesses" for purposes of the act. Specifically, it requires that businesses be (1) independently owned and operated; (2) not dominant in their fields of operation; and (3) meet any "size standards" that the SBA may establish based on the number of employees, dollar volume of business, net worth, net income, or "other appropriate factors."[185] These basic criteria have not changed significantly since the act's enactment in 1958,[186] although the 112th Congress imposed certain requirements upon the SBA's promulgation of regulations revising, modifying, or establishing size standards.[187]

At least one measure in the 113th Congress would amend the definition of *small business* to exclude "publicly traded" firms, "foreign-owned" firms, and their subsidiaries.[188] These entities are not expressly disqualified from recognition as small businesses under the Small Business Act at present, although existing restrictions on firm size and the citizenship of firm owners may effectively exclude at least some of them.[189]

---

[185] 15 U.S.C. §632(a)(1)-(2).

[186] *See* P.L. 85-536, §2, 72 Stat. 384. The Small Business Act of 1953, which established the SBA as a temporary agency, included similar provisions. *See* P.L. 83-163, §203, 67 Stat. 233 (July 30, 1953).

[187] P.L. 112-239, §1661, 126 Stat. 2083-2084. This legislation also prohibits the SBA from limiting the number of size standards, and from establishing or approving a single size standard for a grouping of 4-digit North American Industry Classification System (NAICS) codes unless the SBA justifies that such a standard is appropriate for each industry classification included within the grouping. *Id.* The limitations on SBA's authority to establish single size standards for multiple NAICS codes, in particular, are intended to address issues such as those raised by the SBA's recently proposed grouping of architect and engineer services. Applying the same standards to architect and engineering firms would reportedly have resulted in 97.8% of all architecture firms qualifying as small under the SBA's proposed size standard. *See, e.g.*, Committee Members Introduce Additional Legislation to Reform Small Business Contracting, Feb. 8, 2012, *available at* http://smallbusiness house.gov/News/DocumentSingle.aspx?DocumentID=278695; *Objections to Proposed Size Standard Change Raised at House Small Business Hearing*, 95 FED. CONT. REP. 484 (May 10, 2011).

[188] Fairness and Transparency in Contracting Act, H.R. 1622, §3 (establishing a new definition of *independently owned and operated* that excludes these types of firms).

[189] Currently, the regulations implementing the Small Business Act provide that the SBA generally "counts the receipts, employees, or other measure of size of the concern whose size is at issue and all of its domestic and foreign affiliates, regardless of whether the affiliates are organized for profit." 13 C.F.R. §121.103(a)(6). *See also* 13 C.F.R. §121.103(a)(1) ("Concerns and entities are affiliates of each other when one controls or has the power to control the other, or a third party or parties controls or has the power to control both. It does not matter whether control is exercised, so long as the power to control exists."). Many, although not all, of the set-aside programs similarly limit eligibility to U.S. citizen owners. *See, e.g.*, 13 C.F.R. §124.101 (8(a) Program); 13 C.F.R. §126.200(a) (HUBZone program); 13 C.F.R. §127.200(a)-(b) (women-owned small business program). The Office of Legal Counsel at the Department of Justice has opined that the SBA regulations limiting eligibility for the 8(a) Program to citizens do not deprive resident aliens of due process in violation of the Fifth Amendment to the U.S. Constitution. *See* U.S. Dep't of Justice, Office of Legal Counsel, Constitutionality of 13 C.F.R. §124.103 Establishing Citizenship Requirement for Participation in 8(a) Program, March 4, 1996, *available at* http://www.justice.gov/olc/sba8 htm.

The proposed legislation would also impose related requirements to ensure that agencies and contractors are aware of these changes and the penalties for misrepresentation of business size and status.[190] It also would permit interested parties to file complaints with the SBA and the procuring agencies regarding firms' size or status, and require these complaints to be resolved in a "timely manner."[191] Entities found to have fraudulently misrepresented their size or status would be debarred from government contracts for five years.[192]

Agency-Specific Provisions

The existing laws and proposed legislation discussed thus far generally have government-wide applicability. However, there are other measures that pertain only to an individual agency and, as a general matter, impose more stringent requirements upon that agency than apply to other agencies.[193] Perhaps the most notable example is the Veterans Benefits, Health Care, and Information Technology Act (VBHCITA) of 2006. Sections 502 and 503 of VBHCITA have been construed as generally requiring the VA to set aside contracts for service-disabled veteran-owned small businesses and other veteran-owned small businesses whenever the "Rule of Two" is satisfied.[194] Other agencies are also subject to similar agency-specific requirements as to small business contracting.

---

[190] Fairness and Transparency in Contracting Act, H.R. 1622, §§4 & 7.

[191] *Id.* at §8.

[192] *Id.* at §9. Currently, regulations establish procedures whereby questions about certain firms' size or status may be brought to the SBA. *See, e.g.*, 13 C.F.R. §124.112(c) ("Upon receipt of specific and credible information alleging that a Participant no longer meets the eligibility requirements for continued program eligibility, SBA will review the concern's eligibility for continued participation in the program."). However, such provisions generally do not require the SBA to investigate in a "timely manner," and similar provisions are not made for all set-aside programs. For more on debarment, see generally CRS Report RL34753, *Debarment and Suspension of Government Contractors: A Legal Overview*, by Kate M. Manuel.

[193] *See, e.g.*, 42 U.S.C. §4370d (requiring the Environmental Protection Agency to ensure that at least 8% of federal funding for prime contracts and subcontracts awarded "in support of authorized programs, including grants, loans, and contracts for wastewater treatment and leaking underground storage tanks grants" be made available to small businesses owned and controlled by socially and economically disadvantaged individuals or Historically Black Colleges and Universities); 51 U.S.C. §30304 (requiring the National Aeronautics and Space Administration to establish as a goal that at least 8% of the total value of prime contracts and subcontracts awarded annually in support of certain programs be made to small businesses or other organizations owned or controlled by socially and economically disadvantaged individuals). As discussed previously, the government-wide goal for the percentage of prime contract and subcontract dollars awarded to small disadvantaged businesses is generally 5%, and agency goals have historically paralleled the government-wide goals. *See supra* Government-Wide and Agency-Specific Goals.

[194] P.L. 109-461, 120 Stat. 3431 (Dec. 22, 2006) (codified, in part, at 38 U.S.C. §§8127-8128). Section 502's provisions as to set-asides, in particular, use the word "shall," which has generally been construed to mean that the VA is required to set aside contracts for service-disabled veteran-owned small businesses and other veteran-owned small businesses under Section 502 whenever the Rule of Two is satisfied. *But see* Kingdomware Techs., Inc. v. United States, 107 Fed. Cl. 226 (2012) (upholding the VA's determination to procure certain items through the Federal Supply Schedules, rather than through a set-aside for veteran-owned small businesses); Alternative Contracting Enterprises, LLC; Pierce First Med., B-406265,B-406266,B-406291,B-406291.2,B-406318.1,B-406318.2,B-406343,B-406356,B-406357,B-406369,B-406371,B-406374,B-406400,B-406404,B-406428 (Mar. 26, 2012) (upholding the VA's determination to procure certain items through the AbilityOne Program, rather than through a set-aside for veteran-owned small businesses). By comparison, the Small Business Act authorizes—but does not require—all executive branch agencies to set aside contracts for service-disabled veteran-owned small businesses when the "Rule of Two" is satisfied. Similarly, the Small Business Act does not authorize set-asides for small businesses owned by veterans who are not service-disabled. *See supra **Table 1***.

VA's "Veterans First" Contracting Program

Implemented under the authority of Sections 502 and 503 of VBHCITA, the VA's "Veterans First" contracting program gives small businesses owned by veterans (and certain surviving spouses of veterans) that meet eligibility requirements "preference" in the award of VA contracts. Under Section 502, in particular, the Veterans First program is subject to its own requirements as to (1) goals for contracting with veteran-owned small businesses;[195] (2) set-asides and sole-sources awards to service-disabled veteran-owned small businesses and other veteran-owned small businesses;[196] (3) priority in awards among different types of small businesses;[197] (4) eligibility criteria for firms and owners;[198] and (5) sanctions for misrepresentation of size or status.[199]

Many of these requirements were part of VBHCITA, as originally enacted. However, the 111th Congress substantially amended VBHCITA's eligibility requirements by barring the inclusion of persons whose status had not been verified by the VA in the VA's database of eligible firms and owners.[200] The 112th Congress further amended VBHCITA's penalty provisions by changing the type of actionable conduct from "misrepresentations" of status, to "willful and intentional misrepresentations" of status.[201] The 112th Congress also prescribed a five-year term of debarment from VA contracts for such misrepresentations, instead of leaving the term of any debarment to the VA's discretion. Debarment proceedings must also be commenced and completed within specified timeframes.[202]

Members of the 113th Congress have proposed additional changes to the Veterans First program, including moving responsibility for verifying the status of firms and owners from the VA to the SBA.[203] This legislation would require the SBA to (1) enter into an agreement with the VA transferring "control and administration" of VA's "Veterans First" contracting program to the SBA, subject to certain conditions; (2) assume responsibility for the database that the VA uses in verifying the eligibility of firms and owners; and (3) hear appeals of denials of verifications.[204] The VA, in turn, would also be required to reimburse the SBA for the functions that the SBA performs.[205]

---

[195] 38 U.S.C. §8127(a). Section 502 further requires the VA to establish a "review mechanism" to ensure that subcontracts counted toward the VA's goals are "actually awarded" to a qualifying business. *Id.*

[196] 38 U.S.C. §8127(b)-(d). Under these provisions, the VA is generally required to set aside contracts whose value exceeds the simplified acquisition threshold (generally $150,000) for veteran-owned small businesses if the Rule of Two is satisfied. However, the VA also has discretion to make sole-source awards of contracts (1) whose value is below the simplified acquisition threshold, or (2) whose value exceeds the simplified acquisition threshold, but is below $5 million, provided that the Rule of Two is *not* satisfied.

[197] 38 U.S.C. §8127(*i*)(1)-(4). For further discussion of priority, see *infra* note 210 and accompanying text.

[198] 38 U.S.C. §8127(e), (f), & (h). For further discussion, see *infra* note 206.

[199] 38 U.S.C. §8127(g). Among other things, these provisions establish a mandatory statutory debarment for persons who "willfully and intentionally misrepresent their status." *See infra* note 201 and accompanying text.

[200] Veterans' Benefits Act of 2010, P.L. 111-275, tit. I, §104(b)(1)-(2), 124 Stat. 2867-68 (Oct. 13, 2010).

[201] Honoring America's Veterans and Caring for Camp Lejeune Families Act of 2012, P.L. 112-154, tit. VII, §706, 126 Stat. 1206 (Aug. 6, 2012).

[202] *Id.*

[203] *See supra* notes 204-205 and accompanying text.

[204] H.R. 2882, at §3; H.R. 4435, as reported in the House, §812(c).

[205] H.R. 2882, at §§3-4.

Several other measures introduced in the 113th Congress would expand the circumstances in which family members of veterans may participate in the Veterans First program. Currently, only surviving spouses of veterans with service-connected disabilities rated as 100% disabling, or of veterans who die as the result of a service-connected disability, may participate in the program for a limited period of time.[206] However, under legislation proposed in the 113th Congress, surviving spouses of veterans who have service-connected disabilities rated at less than 100% disabling who do not die from a service-connected disability could participate for a period of time.[207] Surviving spouses or dependents of members of the armed services killed in the line of duty would also be eligible to participate for a period of time.[208]

Other legislation would modify the procedures for making awards under the Veterans First program. One measure would, for example, generally require consideration of whether veteran-owned firms are *local contractors*—a term which would be defined to mean contractors who have principal offices or "locations" within a 60-mile radius of a VA facility—in the award of contracts for the construction or maintenance of VA facilities.[209] The measure would also restate the order of priority for the award of contracts under the Veterans First program. Currently, this order is (1) service-disabled veteran-owned small businesses; (2) veteran-owned small businesses; (3) small disadvantaged businesses and HUBZone small businesses awarded contracts under the authority of Sections 8(a) or 31 of the Small Business Act; and (4) small businesses awarded contracts under other authority (e.g., women-owned small businesses awarded contracts under the authority of Section 8(m) of the Small Business Act).[210] However, the measure introduced in the 113th Congress would change this order of priority to give local small businesses a preference over other small businesses within the same category (i.e., local service-disabled veteran-owned small businesses would have priority other service-disabled veteran-owned small businesses, which would, in turn, have priority over local veteran-owned small businesses, etc.).[211]

Another measure would require the application of "limitations on subcontracting"—or restrictions on the amount of work that prime contractors may subcontract to other entities, rather than perform themselves—to contracts awarded under the authority of VBHCITA.[212] Currently, these limitations apply only to contracts awarded under the authority of the Small Business Act.[213] The Small Business Act grants the Administrator of the SBA the authority to impose similar

---

[206] 38 U.S.C. §8127(h) (generally permitting the surviving spouses of veterans who had service-connected disabilities rated 100% disabling, or who died as a result of service-connected disabilities, to participate in the Veterans First program until the earliest of the following: (1) the date on which the surviving spouse remarries; (2) the date on which the surviving spouse relinquishes an ownership interest in the small business; or (3) the date that is 10 years after the date of the veteran's death).

[207] *See, e.g.*, Service-Disabled Veteran Owned Small Business Relief Act, H.R. 3098, §2; Veterans Small Business Opportunity and Protection Act of 2013, S. 430, §2. The term of participation for surviving spouses of veterans who have service-connected disabilities rated at less than 100% and do not die from a service-connected disability would generally be 3 years, not 10.

[208] *See* Veterans Small Business Opportunity and Protection Act of 2013, S. 430, §3.

[209] *See* Preference for Local Veteran Contractors Act, H.R. 2358, §2.

[210] 38 U.S.C. §8127(*i*)(1)-(4).

[211] *See* Preference for Local Veteran Contractors Act, H.R. 2358, §2.

[212] *See* Protecting Business Opportunities for Veterans Act, H.R. 4281, §2.

[213] *See* 15 U.S.C. §657s(a) (generally requiring that small businesses awarded contracts under the authority of the Small Business Act perform work representing at least 50% of the amounts paid to them under the under the contract themselves or subcontract the work to a "similarly situated entity" (i.e., another small business).

limitations on contracts awarded to small businesses under other authority, but the Administrator does not appear to have done so to date.[214]

Other Agency-Specific Provisions

Other measures enacted or introduced in the 113th Congress similarly address contracting and subcontracting with small businesses by individual agencies. Several measures that have already been enacted provide for individual agencies to be exempted from certain generally applicable requirements as to small business contracting and subcontracting. Perhaps the most notable of these, discussed above, is Section 318 of the Consolidated Appropriations Act (P.L. 113-76). Section 318 permits the DOE to count *first-tier subcontracts* awarded by contractors managing and operating national laboratories toward the DOE and government-wide goals for *prime contracts*.[215] Other measures exempted agencies from similar requirements when contracting with small businesses.[216]

Additional measures that have not been enacted, however, would require additional reporting regarding an agency's performance in contracting with small businesses,[217] or task specific agency officials with certain responsibilities as to contracting with small businesses.[218] One measure would also repeal the provision permitting the DOE to count certain subcontracts toward the DOE and government-wide prime contract goals.[219] Another measure would extend the

---

[214] *See* 15 U.S.C. §657s(d)(1) (authorizing the SBA to impose similar limitations on contracts not awarded under the authority of the Small Business Act by promulgating regulations to this effect).

[215] *See supra* note 26 and accompanying text.

[216] P.L. 113-66, §1615, 127 Stat. 950 (exempting contracts that are subject to limitations on subcontracting pursuant to the Small Business Act from certain requirements as to the review and justification of "pass-through" contracts under Section 802 of the National Defense Authorization Act for Fiscal Year 2013); P.L. 113-76, §7057(h),—Stat.— (permitting the U.S. Agency for International Development (USAID) to provide an exception to the fair opportunity process for placing task orders under such contracts when the order is placed with any category of small or small disadvantaged business). A *pass-through* contract is one where a contractor adds "no, or negligible, value" to the work performed, instead arranging for it to be subcontracted. *See generally* 10 U.S.C. §2324 note (requiring the promulgation of regulations to address "excessive pass-through charges"). USAID has been granted such authority for a number of years. However, such authority may have less significance since the enactment of P.L. 111-240, which generally permits agencies to set aside orders under multiple-award contracts notwithstanding the "fair opportunity" requirements. *See supra* note 89-91.

[217] *See, e.g.*, Transportation Security Acquisition Reform Act, H.R. 2719, §3; & S. 1893, §3 (requiring the Transportation Security Administration to submit to specified congressional committees a report restating the Administration's published goals for contracting with small businesses; its performance record with respect to these goals during the prior fiscal year; an itemized list of challenges in meeting the goals; and an action plan for addressing these challenges).

[218] *See* DHS Acquisition Accountability and Efficiency Act, H.R. 4228, §104 (tasking the Department of Homeland Security Chief Acquisition Officer with responsibility for (1) collecting baseline data and establishing performance measures as to the impact of strategic sourcing on small businesses and (2) ensuring that a "fair proportion" of contract and subcontract dollars is awarded to small businesses, opportunities for small business participation are "maximized," and small businesses that achieve qualified vendor status for security-related technologies are given the opportunity to compete).

[219] *See* Greater Opportunities for Small Business Act, H.R. 4093, §2(a) (repealing Section 15(g)(3) of the Small Business Act, which permits the DOE to count first-tier subcontracts awarded by its management and operating contractors toward the DOE and government-wide prime contracting goals); House Rules Committee Amendment No. 56, to H.R. 4435, as passed by the House, House of Representatives Committee on Rules, H.R. 4435, *available at* http://rules.house.gov/bill/113/hr-4435; House Armed Services Committee, FY15-H.R. 4435 Floor Amendments and Tracker, *available at* http://armedservices.house.gov/index.cfm?p=fy15-h-r-4435-floor-amendments-and-tracker (same).

Department of Defense's Comprehensive Subcontracting Test Program through the end of FY2017.[220] Initially authorized in 1989, this program authorizes the negotiation, administration, and reporting of subcontracting plans on a plant, division, or company-wide basis (rather than on the basis of individual contracts) as a way of assessing whether such "comprehensive" plans may increase subcontracting opportunities for small businesses and reduce administrative burdens on prime contractors.[221]

Author Contact Information

Kate M. Manuel
Legislative Attorney
kmanuel@crs.loc.gov, 7-4477

Acknowledgments

CRS Legislative Attorney Erika K. Lunder co-authored an earlier report, CRS Report R42390, *Federal Contracting and Subcontracting with Small Businesses: Issues in the 112th Congress.*

---

[220] National Defense Authorization Act for FY2015, H.R. 4435, as reported in the House, §811 (changing the expiration date from December 31, 2014, to December 31, 2017). The proposed legislation would also make certain changes to the program, including (1) requiring that comprehensive plans include terms obligating the contractor to report semi-annually on specified information (e.g., costs incurred in negotiating, complying with, and reporting on comprehensive subcontracting plans); (2) requiring that failure to comply with a plan be a "factor considered" in past performance evaluations; (3) requiring the Secretary of Defense to report on the results of the program by the end of FY2015; and (4) incorporating a definition of *covered small business concern* that includes all types of small businesses eligible for set-asides and sole-source awards under the authority of the Small Business Act. The Senate version of the National Defense Authorization Act reportedly would also reauthorize the Comprehensive Subcontracting Test Program, although it is unclear for how long. *See* U.S. Senate Committee on Armed Services, Senate Committee on Armed Services Completes Markup of the National Defense Authorization Act for Fiscal Year 2015, May 23, 2014, at pg. 36, *available at* http://www.armed-services.senate.gov/imo/media/doc/SASC%20NDAA%20markup%20release%2005-23-14.pdf.

[221] National Defense Authorization Act for FY1990 and 1991, P.L. 101-189, §834, 103 Stat. 1509-1510 (Nov. 29, 1989) (codified, as amended, at 15 U.S.C. §637 note).

www.ingramcontent.com/pod-product-compliance
Lightning Source LLC
Chambersburg PA
CBHW080637290526
45790CB00007B/3096